Train Your Board (and Everyone Else) to Raise Money

A Cookbook of Easy-to-Use Fundraising Exercises

The Gold Standard in Books for Your Board

Each Can be Read in One Hour • Generous Discounts Available

Fund Raising Realities Every Board Member Must Face, 2nd Ed.
David Lansdowne,
109 pp., $24.95.

After spending just one hour with this book, board members everywhere will understand virtually everything they need to know about raising major gifts. Among the top three bestselling fundraising books of all time.

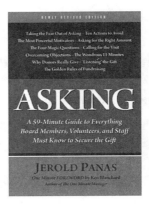

Asking
Jerold Panas, 108 pp., $24.95.

It ranks up there with public speaking. Nearly all of us fear it. Yet it's critical to the success of our organizations. Asking for money. It doesn't take steller sales skills to be an effective asker. Nearly everyone can do it if they follow Jerold Panas' step-by-step guidelines.

The Ultimate Board Member's Book
Kay Sprinkel Grace,
110 pp., $24.95.

A book for all nonprofit boards: those wanting to operate with maximum efficiency, those needing to clarify exactly what their job is, and those wanting to ensure that all members are "on the same page." It's all here in jargon-free language.

The Fundraising Habits of Supremely Successful Boards
Jerold Panas, 108 pp., $24.95.

Jerold Panas has observed more boards at work than perhaps anyone in America, all the while helping them to surpass their goals of $100,000 to $1 million. Here he shares what he has learned about boards that excel at resource development.

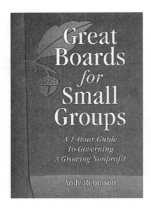

Great Boards for Small Groups
Andy Robinson
109 pp., $24.95.

Does your board need clearly defined objectives, meetings with more focus, broader participation in fundraising, more follow-through between meetings? Say hello to your guide Andy Robinson, who offers fog-burning advice like no other board consultant.

How to Make Your Board Dramatically More Effective, Starting Today
Gayle Gifford, 114 pp., $24.95.

How do you transform a good board into a great one? You have your board ask themselves the right questions. Questions like: Does our vision matter? Are we having an impact? Is our organization worthy of support? Gayle Gifford examines each key question.

Fundraising Mistakes that Bedevil All Boards (and Staff Too)
Kay Sprinkel Grace,
109 pp., $24.95.

Fundraising mistakes are a thing of the past. If you blunder from now on, it's simply evidence you haven't read Grace's book, in which she exposes the 44 costly errors that thwart us time and time again.

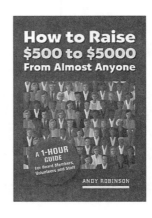

How to Raise $500 to $5000 From Almost Anyone
Andy Robinson, 109 pp., $24.95.

It's true. You can raise $500 to $5000 from practically anyone by following Andy Robinson's advice. He's been in the trenches. He knows what works. Andy pulls no punches while at the same time according great respect to donors.

www.emersonandchurch.com

TRAIN YOUR
BOARD
(And Everyone Else)
TO RAISE
MONEY

A Cookbook of Easy-to-Use Fundraising Exercises

Andrea Kihlstedt
Andy Robinson

Emerson & Church
PUBLISHERS

First printed in March 2014

Printed in the United States of America

ISBN 978-1-889102-51-1

10 9 8 7 6 5

This text is printed on acid-free paper.

Copies of this book are available from the publisher
at discount when purchased in quantity for boards
of directors or staff.

Emerson & Church, Publishers
15 Brook Street • Medfield, MA 02052
Tel. 508-359-0019 • www.emersonandchurch.com

Library of Congress Cataloging-in-Publication Data

Kihlstedt, Andrea.
  Train your board (and everyone else) to raise money : a cookbook of easy-to-use
fundraising exercises / Andrea Kihlstedt and Andy Robinson.
     pages cm
  ISBN 978-1-889102-51-1 (pbk. : alk. paper) 1. Fund raising. 2. Nonprofit
organizations—Finance. 3. Charities—Finance. 4. Boards of directors. I. Robinson,
Andy, 1957- II. Title.
  HG177.K5134 2014
  658.15'224—dc23
                              2013047497

Table of Contents

INTRODUCTION

No one is born knowing how to raise money, but most of us learn to ask for things early in life. We develop a remarkable array of skills to request what we need.

Think about it. You ask all the time. For something to eat or drink. Advice. A date. A job or a raise. A favor. Perhaps a little compassion and understanding. These requests are the glue that holds our communities together. They happen so regularly, we forget how often we ask.

Asking people for money is a bit more complicated. You're not asking for yourself, but rather for your organization. Sometimes you're talking to someone you know; other times not. You might be seeking an amount determined by someone else, and perhaps that amount makes you uncomfortable. Then there's the "money taboo"—the widely held belief that talking about money is impolite or even offensive. It's easy to understand why fundraising makes so many people so uncomfortable.

Here's the good news: with effective training and preparation, anyone can learn to raise money. That's the reason we assembled this book.

You can start with brief exercises to begin board meetings, then add practice sessions before the annual fund campaign or occasional workshops or training retreats. Taken together, your efforts will increase everyone's comfort and improve their skills.

You don't have to be a professional trainer to use this book effectively. If you need to raise money for your organization—and you want more people to help—well, we wrote this book for you.

How to Use This Book

These exercises have been designed primarily to train board members, but they'll also work with staff, your development committee or campaign committee, or other volunteers. You can combine them in different ways to train just about anyone to raise more money.

Each chapter's activities address a particular topic in fundraising, starting with the most general and then focusing on specific aspects of planning and donor engagement. Where appropriate, we have suggested exercises you might use together because they naturally follow one another. We've also created several exercise menus (see page 10) you can use to serve different purposes.

Use this book to create a training plan that complements your fundraising calendar. Early in the year, for example—as your fundraising is gearing up— you can devote fifteen minutes at a board meeting to one of the introductory exercises, such as Why People Give or What Are We Afraid Of? If your board members don't know each other well, consider some of the continuum activities outlined in Where Do You Stand? Before kicking off your fall major gifts campaign, use the solicitor training exercises to prepare staff, board, and volunteers to meet with donors.

You might think of this as a training cookbook. Each exercise has a brief introduction, a list of ingredients, instructions for facilitating the activity, and a training tip to help improve your skills. We hope you'll return to it again and again, like a good cookbook, trying out new exercises and reusing old ones as you fine-tune them to fit your training style and your organization.

Suggested Menus

We've created these menus to help you easily find exercises that will address your organization's specific challenges and take advantage of fundraising opportunities. We encourage you to adapt these menus to fit your tastes and training preferences.

Give Confidence to the Fundraising-Phobic
  What Are We Afraid Of?
  Why Do You Care?
  Things You Learned About Money as a Child
  Where's the Money?
  Why People Give
  Fundraising on Faith

Get Everyone Involved in Fundraising
  Cycle of Fundraising
  Fundraising Effectiveness Quiz
  What's Our Mission?
  Building a Board Fundraising Ladder
  The Gift Is Just the Beginning

Help People Tell Your Story (and Theirs)
  The Case, Simplified
  Making Headlines
  Features and Benefits: What Are We Selling?
  One Minute of Fame
  Six-Word Stories
  Trust Your Instincts: Six Quick Asks
  Your Favorite Thanks

Engage Volunteers in Shaping Your Fundraising Program
  Cycle of Fundraising
  Fundraising Effectiveness Quiz
  Building a Gift Chart
  Creating a Twelve-Week Major Gifts Campaign
  The ABCs of Identifying Prospects
  Rating Your Prospects (Pizza and Beer)
  Creating a Board Fundraising Menu
  Planning a Fundraising House Party

Engage Your Current Supporters

    Cycle of Fundraising

    Active Listening: What Did You Hear?

    Instant Donor

    Shall We Meet? Overcoming Objections by Phone

    Face-to-Face Fundraising: Structuring the Meeting

    Trio Ask

    After the Yes: Questions You Can Ask Donors

    How Many Relationships Can You Manage?

New Board Member Training

    What's Our Mission?

    What Drew You to This Work?

    Where's the Money?

    Cycle of Fundraising

A Calendar of Exercises for Monthly Board Meetings

January	Features and Benefits: What Are We Selling?
February	Why People Give
March	Instant Donor
April	Where's the Money?
May	Cycle of Fundraising
June	Fundraising Effectiveness Quiz
July	The Case, Simplified
August	The ABCs of Identifying Prospects
September	Fundraising on Steroids: A Fundraising Game
October	Board Giving: What's the Right Amount?
November	Trust Your Instincts: Six Quick Asks
December	Your Favorite Thanks

Agenda for a Full-Day Board Retreat

    Where Do You Stand? Fundraising Continuums

    Things You Learned About Money as a Child

    Where's the Money?

    Cycle of Fundraising

    Why People Give

    The ABCs of Identifying Prospects

    The Case, Simplified

    Trio Ask

    Thanking Donors from A to Z

Agenda for a Half-Day Board Workshop
>Features and Benefits: What Are We Selling?
>Why People Give
>Cycle of Fundraising
>Creating a Board Fundraising Menu
>Trust Your Instincts: Six Quick Asks

Train Your Program Staff about Fundraising
>If Money Wasn't Scarce
>Where's the Money?
>Features and Benefits: What Are We Selling?
>Fundraising Effectiveness Quiz
>Thanking Donors from A to Z

Prepare for Your Major Gifts Campaign
>Creating a Twelve-Week Major Gifts Campaign
>How Many Relationships Can You Manage?
>Donors All Around Us
>Face-to-Face Fundraising: Structuring the Meeting
>Closing the Gift
>Shall We Meet? Overcoming Objections by Phone
>Trio Ask
>After the Yes: Questions You Can Ask Donors

Prepare for a House Party
>Planning a Fundraising House Party
>Fundraising House Parties: Engaging Your Board
>Pitching in Public

Quick and Easy: 20 Minutes or Less
>Where Do You Stand? Fundraising Continuums
>Why Do You Care?
>Things You Learned About Money as a Child
>What Are We Afraid Of?
>Why People Give
>Where's the Money?
>Fundraising on Faith
>Fundraising Effectiveness Quiz
>What Drew You to This Work?
>What's Our Mission?
>Features and Benefits: What Are We Selling?
>Six-Word Stories
>Board Giving: What's the Right Amount?

Your Toolbox and Icons

To facilitate the exercises in this book, you'll need a basic trainer's tool kit.

A timer. You can use a stopwatch, wristwatch, or your smartphone.

A noisemaker. Use a bell, chime, or train whistle to get people's attention. It should be loud enough to be heard over lots of voices.

A sturdy easel and flip chart. Self-adhesive flip chart paper is handy. If you don't have that, get a roll of painter's tape that won't pull paint off the wall.

A set of multicolored markers. Choose water-based markers (less smelly) with broad nibs. Test them to make sure they are fresh.

Tape. Unless you're using self-stick flip chart paper, tape is helpful. We recommend painter's tape, which won't pull paint off the wall.

Paper and pens are required for some exercises.

We've placed small icons at the beginning of each exercise so you can see at a glance how long it will take and what facilitation tools you'll need.

Stopwatch. Any sort of timer will do: wristwatch, egg timer, smartphone.

Advance preparation. For some activities, you'll need to prepare flip charts in advance, photocopy materials, or do other homework.

Capital campaign. These activities are particularly helpful for organizations planning a capital campaign.

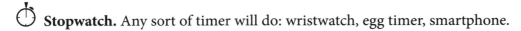

Experienced fundraiser. Most activities in this book can be led by anyone, but some require a basic understanding of fundraising.

Bell. Use your favorite noisemaker—bell, whistle, a fork clinking on a glass.

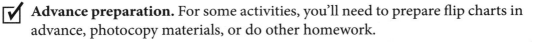

Movement. Several exercises require people to move around.

Flip chart. A whiteboard or smart board can readily substitute, although some exercises require you to post paper in several locations around the room.

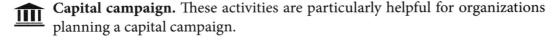

Worksheets, paper, and pens. We have prepared worksheets for several activities; you'll find them in the book following the relevant exercises. Photocopy them from the book or create your own using the templates we've provided.

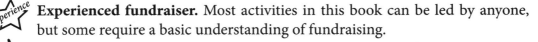

00:15   **Time.** Look for the digital clock face. These are estimates; as the advertisements say, your results may vary.

Fundraising Basics

 You don't have to be a fundraising expert to use this book. Most of these exercises can be facilitated by anyone. But there are some activities which we believe an experienced fundraiser should lead. For these we've included a special icon.

Here is some general information about fundraising to keep in mind.

There is plenty of money available. Nonprofits in the United States raise a total of $1.5 trillion each year from three sources: earned income from service fees and product sales, government grants and contracts, and philanthropy. The philanthropic slice of the pie, which includes gifts from individuals, foundations, and corporations, totals more than $300 billion per year.

Most philanthropy comes from individuals. Year after year, about 80% of donated dollars are given by individuals. People new to fundraising tend to think it's all about foundation grants and corporate gifts, but these comprise only 20% of private giving. Indeed, through their bequests and estate plans, deceased donors give more money annually than all U.S. corporations combined.

Most people give. Seven out of ten households contribute to charitable organizations. Further, a large proportion of charitable dollars are given by middle class, working class, and poor people. Many novices wrongly believe that fundraising is about trying to identify and ask rich strangers.

People give because they are asked. Indeed, academics have conducted research about why people don't give, and the number one reason is "Nobody asked."

The most effective way to ask is face to face. Unfortunately, this is also the scariest way. Many of the exercises included here are designed to help people get over their fear, build their skills and confidence, and get out and ask.

It's all about relationships. Fundraising isn't just asking for money. It's a whole suite of behaviors that include identifying donors, cultivating them, asking for support, recognizing them when they give, and involving them in your work. Several exercises in this book will help you work through the nuts and bolts of maintaining mutually rewarding relationships with your donors.

Getting Started as a Trainer

Each exercise in this book includes a tip to help you develop your training and facilitation skills. The following suggestions apply to all the exercises and are frankly applicable to almost any situation where people gather to learn new skills and learn from each other.

1. **You don't have to be an expert.** Sure, it's easier to train people to raise money if you know something about fundraising, but most of these exercises are designed to work with trainers (and audiences) of any skill level.

   If you're asked a question you can't answer, it's perfectly fine to say, "Martha, that's a great question. I don't know the answer." When in doubt, remember the old trainer trick: pass it back to the group— "Who has a good response?"

   If you're a novice trainer, it's useful to acknowledge that: "This is my first time leading this exercise, so I'll need everyone to help me out, okay?"

2. **Honor your need (or not) for preparation.** Some people prepare rigorously before trying something new; others jump in. We've done our best to design these exercises for people who land anywhere along the "preparation continuum." If you need to thoroughly prepare in advance, please do. And if you're comfortable opening the book, reading an exercise, and facilitating it in real time, go for it.

3. **People remember what *they* do, not what *you* say.** This is the heart of adult learning theory, which is why this book is a series of activities, role plays, and games, not lectures or PowerPoint slides. As noted earlier, you don't have to be a fundraising expert to lead the exercises— you just have to facilitate the group.

4. **Pay attention to logistics.** The success or failure of a training event depends, in large measure, on people's physical comfort.

   - If possible, *position the chairs so people can talk to each other—* around a table, for example—rather than classroom style or in a large U with people far apart. For many of these exercises, an informal circle of chairs will work well.

- *Choose a room with good light*, preferably natural light.
- *Set the thermostat* to a comfortable temperature. If you're concerned, poll the group—"Is anyone else cold?"—and adjust accordingly.
- *Create good sight lines* so people can see what you're writing on the flip chart.
- *Avoid glare.* Never have the audience facing large windows during the daytime. You (and your easel) will be backlit and difficult to see.
- *Use big markers that don't smell.* Some markers are pretty toxic, and your colleagues may have chemical sensitivities.
- *Write visibly.* Use letters that are large enough so everyone can see clearly. Not sure how big is big enough? Write something, then sit in the farthest chair. Can you read it easily?
- *Use red, pink, orange, and yellow only as accent colors.* They aren't as visible as blue, green, brown, purple, and black.
- *Speak up.* Project your voice. Make it carry. Learn to speak from the core of your body, rather than relying entirely on your throat. Ask everyone else to speak up, too. If the room is large and acoustics poor, you may need to repeat questions (loudly) so everyone can hear them. If you anticipate that people will have trouble hearing you, get a microphone.

5. **Keep things moving: the pace and the people.** If you're a new trainer, you may feel the desire to answer every question and pursue every tangent. We've designed these activities to make it easy to stay on task, but people sometimes raise unrelated topics. It's your job to address people's concerns while keeping the group on track. You can always say, "Let's complete the exercise and then discuss that question when we debrief it together at the end."

If you want to add energy, give people the chance to move. For example, if the exercise calls for work in pairs, encourage everyone to stand up, move around, find a partner, and spread out around the room.

6. **Be supportive.** Reinforce your colleagues by saying things like "What a great question" and "That's a really thoughtful response." Don't be dismissive or make people feel like they're asking dumb questions.

If your group is brainstorming ideas and suggestions, include them all as you write notes on the flip chart. If you selectively include some comments and leave others out, people will feel disrespected and will hesitate to offer more ideas.

7. **Listen to the group and trust where they want to go.** In some ways, this is a contradiction (see item 5 above), but the best facilitators can sense when it's time to follow the group away from the agenda and into the work they really need to do. On this topic, it's best to trust your instincts. If it feels fruitful, go there; if not, stick to the agenda. If you decide to veer off the agenda, make that decision transparently and redesign the agenda on the spot.

8. **Gimmicks are good.** After years of shouting, "Can I get your attention?" Andy finally bought a bell and a train whistle—and they come in handy. Another trick is to make the exercises competitive (several are designed this way) and give out prizes. "The small group that brainstorms the most items in the next three minutes will win a fabulous prize." This always increases the energy level in the room. Note that the best "fabulous prizes" are often inexpensive and silly.

9. **Debrief everything.** Every activity, game, exercise, and contest in this book includes a debriefing: a chance to sit together when it's over and ask, "What did we just learn? How do we apply it?" Sharing these lessons clarifies the value of the exercise, integrates the knowledge, and helps everyone figure out how to apply it. We encourage you to trust the lessons that emerge during these conversations, even if they are not the ones you anticipated at the start of the exercise.

10. **Share the wealth, share the power.** The activities in this book provide an excellent opportunity to develop leadership skills. Once you've facilitated a few of these exercises, encourage your colleagues to take turns at the front of the room.

Feel free to share your stories by sending us an email or visiting our websites:

andreakihlstedt@gmail.com
www.andreakihlstedt.com

andy@andyrobinsononline.com
www.andyrobinsononline.com

Have fun—enjoy yourself!

For more board training material, visit www.trainyourboard.com.

PART 1

Reducing Barriers to Fundraising

One recent morning, while we were working together on this book, the phone rang. Keiren, a fundraising colleague, was calling for advice. She was about to meet with potential donors for her organization and needed some guidance, hand-holding, and encouragement. In a word, she was anxious.

There's nothing unusual about feeling nervous about asking; that's the point of this story. Keiren has been in the fundraising field for more than a decade. She's an experienced, successful professional who has secured gifts large and small. And even she was apprehensive!

This section is dedicated to people uncomfortable with "the ask." In other words, it's for everyone. The section is filled with exercises to ease your anxieties. Most are simple and can be done in a few minutes at the beginning or end of a board meeting. Some are a bit provocative and others are fun—after all, who wouldn't want to explore what it feels like to give away $100,000?

Use these exercises as you see fit. They work particularly well as icebreakers to ease your colleagues into the world of donor fundraising, one step at a time.

Where Do You Stand?
Fundraising Continuums  00:15

When you consider the ubiquitous raffles, benefit events, cookie and candy sales, most of us have far more fundraising experience than we realize. Many people have sales backgrounds and ask for money every day. Others have prepared grant proposals or solicited corporate gifts. The purpose of this activity is to assess the fundraising skill level of your team and to reinforce the idea that your colleagues know more than they think. It's also a fun, physical activity that gets people moving.

Why Do This Exercise?
To uncover useful information about how best to engage members of your fundraising team

Use This Exercise When
You want to address board assumptions about fundraising, or during an early meeting of your development committee, campaign committee, or other fundraising group

Time Required
10 to 20 minutes, depending on the number of questions you ask

Audience
Anyone involved with your fundraising campaign: some combination of board, staff, and volunteers

Setting
A space with enough room for people to move around. If the weather's nice and you have a reasonably quiet location, this activity works well outdoors, too.

Materials
A bell, whistle, or other noisemaker is useful but not essential

FACILITATING THE EXERCISE

1. Ask everyone to stand in one line shoulder to shoulder in random order, facing you.

2. Explain that you'll be asking a series of questions such as, "How many years of experience do you have in fundraising?" and "What's the biggest amount you've ever asked for?" According to the answers they give, participants will then position themselves along the line, those with the most experience standing at one end and those with the least experience at the other. Emphasize that to create the correct sequence they need to talk to each other as they move around: "I have three years of fundraising experience—who has less than that? Who has more?"

3. Sample questions; choose the ones that seem most interesting and relevant.

    - How many years in total have you been doing any sort of fundraising? For your organization, other groups, your church or school, as a staff member or volunteer. (For instance, selling Girl Scout cookies counts.) How many total years?

    - What's the largest amount you've ever asked for face to face? You can include a charitable solicitation, a grant proposal—if you met with the funder in person—or raising money for a business. You can even include asking your parents, but you can't include your mortgage. Notice that the verb is "ask," not "get." What's your largest face-to-face ask?

    - How would you rate your comfort in asking? This end (point to one end of the line) equals deeply uncomfortable. At the other end (point in that direction), asking is no big deal. Where would you stand on the spectrum?

    - In a typical year, how many different nonprofits do you support financially?

    - How would you rate the amount of planning you do as a donor? At one end (point to one end of the line), you tend to give money sponta- neously. At the other end (point), you tend to plan—maybe you even have an estate plan so organizations will benefit when you pass away. Where do you stand?

    - How many hours per month—realistically—do you have available to help with fundraising for our organization?

4. Once you've asked a question and participants settle into their positions along the line, you may need to ring a bell or blow a whistle to get their attention and quiet the conversations. Go down the line, asking each per- son to name their number: number of years, largest ask, level of comfort. You can also call on people as you see fit to provide more detail. "Joe, you say the largest amount you've asked for is $1,000? What was the circumstance?"

    Look for opportunities to draw useful conclusions. For example, "There are ten of us in the room, and we've got more than 100 years of experience among us. I bet we know more about fundraising than we realize." Or try this: "Looks like we have a wide range of available time; some of us can offer only a few hours per month. Maybe we should choose at least a few fundraising strategies that don't require a big time commitment."

5. Once you've commented on responses to one question, ask another. Feel free even to make up your own, but note that this exercise doesn't work with yes-or-no questions. Your questions must allow individuals to rate themselves along a continuum.

6. Ask everyone to return to their seats, then debrief the exercise by asking the following questions:

    •   What did you learn about our group?

    •   What did you learn about your experience and expertise in relation to the other members of the group?

TRAINING TIP Pay attention to everyone's body language. Depending on the number of questions you ask and how talkative people are, this exercise can easily run too long. If you see people starting to sag—leaning against walls, moving away from the line to take a seat, or just physically slumping—look for an opportunity to end the exercise promptly and have everyone return to their seats.

Why Do You Care?

The best board members serve as ambassadors, spreading the word about your organization and its work. When they know what to say, they'll talk more readily with their friends, neighbors, colleagues, and even donors—more readily and more often.

To fill this ambassador role effectively, board members needn't memorize the mission or learn an elevator speech or rehearse the key points of the strategic plan. They just need to articulate why they care. Once they've voiced this, they'll never forget it. And nothing is more powerful than a statement of their own personal commitment.

In addition to finding their own passion and the words to describe it, those who participate in this exercise will come to know each other better, increasing their sense of community and camaraderie.

Why Do This Exercise?
Storytelling is at the heart of fundraising, and people need to be encouraged to tell their stories and the story of your organization

Use This Exercise When
You're building a fundraising team or bringing in new board members or volunteers

Time Required
10 to 15 minutes

Audience
Your board. This exercise also works well for staff and key volunteers.

Setting
A room large enough for your board to move around and mingle. If the weather's nice and you have a reasonably quiet location, this activity works well outdoors, too.

Materials
- Stopwatch and timer
- Bell or whistle
- Paper and pens

FACILITATING THE EXERCISE

1. Hand out paper and pens and ask the following questions:

    - What would you say if someone asked why you cared enough to serve on our board?

- What moves you—really moves you—about our organization and its work? How would you talk about that with other people?

Tell them they will soon share their responses with four other board members and give them a few minutes to make notes.

2. When they've finished writing, describe the exercise as follows. "When I say to begin, please stand up and find a partner. If you don't know the person well, introduce yourself. Then take about thirty seconds each to tell your stories. When I ring the bell, move on to another person. We will do this four times."

3. After four rounds, ask everyone to be seated. Debrief the exercise using some combination of the following questions:

   - What was the experience like?
   - What were your colleagues saying?
   - Was this exercise easy or difficult for you? Why?
   - What did you learn from others?
   - Did you find that your language changed with each new partner? If so, how?
   - Were you surprised by anything you said? Or anything you heard?

4. After the debriefing, summarize any key points. You might comment, for example, on how everyone found it easy to talk about why they care. Or you might note that many mentioned the power of a particular program. Or you might just comment on the energy level in the room and how their enthusiasm was contagious.

5. Conclude the exercise by asking the group for their thoughts about how you might apply the ideas you generated to improve your fundraising.

We thank Gail Perry of Fired Up Fundraising for sharing this exercise.

TRAINING TIP Even with simple exercises like this one, it's helpful to give very clear instructions so everyone knows exactly what's expected. If you're a new facilitator, you might choose to write the instructions or have this book handy.

Things You Learned About Money as a Child

 00:15

Perhaps the greatest barrier to effective fundraising is the discomfort people feel when talking about money. For many of us, it remains a taboo subject. In a simple, non-threatening way, this exercise explores the roots of these money taboos in our own childhoods and makes them, well, less taboo.

Why Do This Exercise?
To help people address their discomfort when discussing money

Use This Exercise When
You're working with a team of inexperienced fundraisers, especially board members

Time Required
10-15 minutes

Audience
Anyone involved with your

fundraising campaign: some combination of board, staff, and volunteers

Setting
A board table or meeting room will work nicely. For a larger training, seat participants at tables in small groups.

Materials
Flip chart paper and markers (optional)

FACILITATING THE EXERCISE

1. Ask your colleagues the following questions, instructing them to raise their hands if they can say yes to any given question:

   - When you were a child, how many of you knew what your parents earned?
   - How many of you know how much money your best friend earns?
   - How many of you talk about money over a family meal?
   - Who's ever had a discussion with a close friend about how you make financial decisions?

   Note how few hands are raised. In our culture, we don't talk very much about money.

2. To explore why the subject of money is so taboo, ask your colleagues to form groups of two or three and discuss what they learned about money as a child. Ask them to come up with three or four ideas, either from hearing

their parents talk about money or from observing how people behaved.

3. After about three minutes, reconvene the full group to debrief the exercise by asking, "What messages did you discuss?" If you like, you can record their answers on the flip chart. Here is a list of the most common messages:

    -   *Money is hard to get.* ("It doesn't grow on trees.")
    -   *Money is dirty.* ("Don't put that in your mouth.")
    -   *Money equals power.* ("When I grow up, I want to be rich.")
    -   *Money corrupts.* (We've all heard the misquoted expression "Money is the root of all evil." The correct verse is, "The love of money …")
    -   *Money is private.* In some cultures, discussing money is more offensive than talking about sex or death.
    -   *Money doesn't buy happiness.*
    -   In many faith traditions, *it's an obligation to give money to others.*

    The most important lesson is this: money is one tool of many you need to do your work. It's neither evil nor sacred, neither good nor bad. The true value of money is how it can be used to create change.

4. If it feels productive, you can extend this exercise during the debriefing period by asking a few additional questions. For example:

    -   Does anyone have a specific story to tell about something you learned about money when you were growing up?
    -   Does anyone have a story about being surprised by a charitable gift you received, or maybe even one you made?

    Here's another great follow-up question that always gets a laugh:

    -   How many of you have children? [Show of hands.] How many of your children have a hard time asking *you* for money?

    You might also ask people, in light of this exercise, what messages they would like their children to learn about money.

We thank our colleague Kim Klein of Klein and Roth Consulting for sharing this exercise.

TRAINING TIP This activity provides a relatively safe way to talk about a delicate subject. Having said that, some people may choose to listen rather than participate, not being willing to share their own experiences.

What Are We Afraid Of?

No matter how many times people ask for money, they're likely to experience that queasy feeling in the pit of their stomachs—the unwelcome sensation that they're somehow putting themselves at risk. This simple exercise helps participants address their fears by giving voice to them and shows that others also experience anxiety about fundraising. People may laugh at their discomfort as they realize the same fears are also common in other parts of their lives.

To ensure that you end your training session on a positive note, we suggest pairing this exercise with the one that follows, Why People Give.

Why Do This Exercise?
Because most of our fears about fundraising are irrational

Use This Exercise When
You're looking for a simple icebreaker to use with inexperienced fundraisers

Time Required
15-20 minutes

Audience
Anyone involved with your fundraising campaign: some combination of board, staff, and volunteers

Setting
A board table, meeting room, or conference room. For a larger training, seat people at tables in small groups.

Materials
Flip chart paper and markers

FACILITATING THE EXERCISE

This exercise should be spontaneous and energetic, without much time for serious reflection.

1. Select someone in advance to write notes on the flip chart, or simply ask for a volunteer from the group.

2. Introduce the exercise by stating that everyone who asks for donations feels some anxiety. While this discomfort will ease with practice, it's nevertheless a central part of the experience. Your goal is to identify and help alleviate the sources of this discomfort.

3. Ask participants to tell you what makes them nervous or anxious about fundraising. Have the scribe write as many as possible. The list will contain many items, including:

   - Fear of rejection
   - Not knowing enough; "I might be asked a question I can't answer"
   - Not knowing the right way to do it
   - Not knowing exactly what to say
   - Not knowing if I'll be successful
   - They won't want to talk to me
   - They won't return my calls
   - Don't want to bring money into our relationship
   - Might impose on people who are unable or unwilling to give

4. Once you have this quick list, ask the group what other aspects of their lives have created similar fears. Most often people will talk about dating, or perhaps asking their employer for a promotion or a raise. Ask them what strategies they used to overcome these fears.

5. Debrief the exercise using some combination of the following questions:

   - Which item on our list is the biggest barrier for you personally? Why?
   - What steps might you take to overcome that barrier?

6. Conclude the discussion by asking for suggestions about how to move forward and ask anyway, despite the natural anxiety accompanying the process.

> **TRAINING TIP** Many exercises work best when they have a spirit of energy and fun. It matters more that the group is energized by the process and less that you've captured every single item for the list. If there's a lull in the flow of ideas, you can always offer one of your own, but be sure not to dominate the group by providing most of the suggestions.

Why People Give

 00:20

One of fundraising's persistent myths is that we pressure people into doing something they don't want to do. Much of our common language reflects this: We "hit people up" for donations; we "target" donors; we "bring in the big guns" to meet with prospects; we "shake people down" and "twist arms" for contributions. Even the word "campaign," which is frequently used to describe a coordinated fundraising effort, comes from the military.

Clearly we need better metaphors. By providing the opportunity for participants to reflect on their own giving and the way it enriches their lives, we begin to change the conversation: people like to give. They enjoy it. It feels good.

Why Do This Exercise?
When people reflect on the value and pleasure of their own giving, they start to realize that asking for contributions is a privilege and not an imposition

Use This Exercise When
Your board and volunteers are resistant to asking and you need to shift their perspective

Time Required
15 to 20 minutes

Audience
Anyone involved with your fundraising campaign: some combination of board, staff, and volunteers

Setting
Anywhere you gather to work on your campaign plan and train your participants

Materials
Flip chart paper and markers

FACILITATING THE EXERCISE

1. Ask your colleagues to form into small groups of three to five to talk about the most meaningful gifts they ever made and why they did so.

2. After about five minutes, reconvene the large group. Debrief their responses by asking, "Why do you give?"

    You'll hear a variety of responses: I believe in the cause, see a need, want to help, giving expresses my values, family tradition, honor someone, tax break. Record these answers on the flip chart. Make a point to share with the group the most important reasons people give:

- They were asked
- They were asked by somebody they know; in other words, the relationship between the giver and the asker
- They feel connected to the work or know someone who has benefited from it
- They want to participate—and making a donation is an easy way to participate

You'll find that people's reasons for giving are deeply ingrained in their beliefs. Their reasons vary widely. They give because they receive something in return. For example, some feel good when they give. Others may sense that they've fulfilled an obligation or have a chance to make a difference in the world. And some may give to return a favor they received in the past.

3. To wrap up the exercise, introduce the idea of the *value for value exchange*. In most monetary transactions, the buyer receives something tangible, like a haircut or a bag of groceries. When people give to nonprofits, the exchange is more subtle but also more powerful. Their generosity helps build a stronger community. They feel good about themselves and see value in the efforts made possible by their support.

    Fundraising is neither begging nor warfare; donors clearly get something in return for their gifts (and we're not talking about coffee mugs or tote bags).

4. To debrief this exercise, use the following questions:

    - Did you hear any responses that surprised you? Which ones? Why?
    - When you think about the organizations you support, how good a job do they do at helping you remember why you give? How could they do better?
    - How can we do a better job with our donors?

We thank our colleague Kim Klein of Klein and Roth Consulting for sharing this exercise.

TRAINING TIP If people bring up negative reasons for giving—guilt, shame, peer pressure—write them down and keep moving. (Whenever the word "guilt" is mentioned, it usually generates a nervous laugh.) By the end of the exercise, you can count positive versus negative motivators and point out how positive, productive reasons far outweigh the negative.

How High Will You Go?

 00:30

Many people give, and continue to give, out of habit. If they give $50 or $500 or even $5,000 to an organization, they're likely to continue at that level until something makes them rethink their giving or reconsider the size of their gifts. In this exercise, without specifically sharing amounts with others, participants will explore how they make charitable choices. The conversation often yields some surprising and useful information.

Why Do This Exercise?
To help people learn what motivates them as donors and apply that learning to others

Use This Exercise When
You want to challenge your board to consider making larger gifts before asking others to give

Time Required
30 minutes

Audience
Anyone involved with your fundraising campaign: some combination of board, staff, and volunteers—though this exercise is especially useful for boards

Setting
A private room, large enough to seat participants in a circle—either around a table or freestanding

Materials
- Flip chart paper and markers
- Paper and pens

FACILITATING THE EXERCISE

1. From the start, it's important to emphasize that you will NOT be asking attendees to reveal the dollar amounts of their giving. You must respect people's privacy as donors, while at the same time encouraging them to share the process they use to determine the size of their gifts.

2. Begin by telling participants that your goal is to help everyone think about how donors make giving decisions. The more they understand the factors that influence gift amounts, the more effective they'll be as solicitors.

3. Ask participants to think of two different gift amounts that represent the high and low of what they might consider giving to your organization this year. If you're about to launch your annual campaign, focus on that. If you're in the middle of a capital campaign, emphasize that.

4. Ask each person to write down three things that would encourage him or her to give at the high end of the range. Then ask everyone to share one or two items, capturing their ideas on the flip chart. They might offer the following ideas:

- If I knew my increased gift would really make a difference
- If I was asked in person
- If my gift was matched by someone else's gift
- If I was clearer about what was expected of me as a board member
- If I felt more connected to the mission

5. When you have completed the list, ask the group for help selecting the three most common reasons. Star or underline these items.

6. To debrief the exercise, ask some combination of the following questions:

- Among the many reasons donors might increase their gifts, which reasons did you find most intriguing? Why?
- When asking for donations, how might we apply these ideas? (For example, you might solicit every board member in person, or seek challenge gifts to be matched by board donations.)
- What are some ways we might incorporate these suggestions into our fundraising and outreach materials?

Please note: while this activity does not emphasize the amount of people's gifts, everyone will be actively thinking about whether they might make a larger contribution.

TRAINING TIP When writing suggestions on the flip chart, be sure to include all of them. If someone duplicates an earlier suggestion, put a check mark by the item you've already written to acknowledge its importance. If you pick and choose ideas, those whose suggestions you don't write down will feel disrespected and hesitate to offer more ideas.

Instant Donor

It's fun to give away money, especially if it doesn't cost you anything. In this exercise, board members get to fantasize about how they would distribute $100,000, an amount far greater than most have had the opportunity to give. Along the way, participants learn about each other's deeply held values in a way that's comfortable, safe, and entertaining.

Why Do This Exercise?
As a solicitor, your most important role is serving as a sounding board for the donor

Use This Exercise When
You want to emphasize that fundraising is more about listening than talking

Time Required
45 minutes

Audience
Anyone involved with your fundraising campaign: some combination of board, staff, and volunteers

Setting
A room large enough for the participants to talk quietly in pairs. Flexible seating is preferred.

Materials
- Stopwatch or timer
- Bell or whistle
- Flip chart paper and markers
- Paper and pens

FACILITATING THE EXERCISE

Sometimes we call this the Fantasy Donor exercise. The premise is that $100,000 has just been deposited into each person's bank account. If you're working with a group for whom $100,000 isn't a lot of money, add some zeros.

1. By way of introduction, tell your participants that they're about to practice giving and listening. Ask everyone to pair up with someone they don't know very well. Tell them they've each been handed $100,000 with the requirement they must give it all away. They may share the money with their family, friends, or any organizations they choose, but they may not create a foundation or use it for any other form of deferred giving. They may *not* use it to buy something like a new car or a trip around the world.

2. Tell them there will be two rounds, with each lasting about seven minutes. During the first round, one person per pair will be the donor and the other will serve as a sounding board for the donor as he or she decides to whom and in what amounts to contribute. During round two, they switch roles.

Clarify that the role of the sounding board is not to advise or convince the donor about how to divvy up the money. Rather, he or she should listen and reflect on what the donor says about giving priorities, amplifying the ideas rather than shaping them. The sounding board might say, "Tell me more about that" or "This is what I hear you saying. Is that right?"

3. Ask people to sit quietly for a few minutes and write out a simple giving plan, including gift recipients and amounts.

4. Ask each pair to choose who will be the donor first and who will be the sounding board. When you ring the bell, the donors discuss their giving plans. After about seven minutes, ring the bell again. At that point, pairs switch roles and spend another seven minutes on this task.

5. At the conclusion of the second round, ask them to discuss the following questions with their partners, allowing three to five minutes:

   • What shaped your giving decisions?
   • What role did your partner play in helping to form those decisions?

6. Pull together the full group. Ask participants to raise their hands if they learned something about their partners they hadn't known before. Ask for a few examples of things they learned. You might comment on the personal nature of philanthropy: the ways our giving decisions are shaped by our own unique experiences. Or, call attention to how giving priorities grow out of deeply held values that relate to our personal history.

7. To debrief the exercise, ask the following additional questions:

   • What does this exercise tell us about the people we're likely to solicit?
   • What can we learn from this exercise about our role as solicitors?
   • What are three things you want to remember from this exercise?

   Ask individuals to write their answers, then encourage everyone to share one or two items from their lists.

Through this exercise, participants learn that all giving is personal. An effective solicitor functions more like a sounding board than a salesperson.

TRAINING TIP Encouraging everyone to write three things they want to remember is an excellent way to wrap up almost any substantive exercise. Participants can create their own meaning from the experience.

PART 2

Debunking Fundraising Myths

In fundraising, like anything else in life, there's a strong tendency to project our experiences and assume others feel as we do. For example:

- "I don't like it when people call me on the phone. Therefore, nobody likes it."
- "I know people who are out of work and would have a hard time giving. Therefore, everyone is broke and no one can give."
- "I prefer to give once per year. Therefore, everyone prefers to give once per year."

If you think about any of these statements, it's easy enough to prove them false. Call centers continue to operate because a certain percentage of people respond. Even during economic recessions, nonprofits raise hundreds of billions each year. Churches and other faith organizations raise the greatest percentage of charitable dollars, and they ask *every week*.

Misconceptions begin from naïveté. If you're new to fundraising, it's normal to make assumptions based on your limited experience. As this section points out exercise by exercise, your assumptions are probably incorrect.

One lesson to keep in mind: organizations must know their supporters well enough to customize the approach for each donor. As a colleague likes to say, "If you know one donor, you know one donor."

Where's the Money?

If you've ever discussed fundraising with your board—or any nonprofit board—you've probably heard the following phrases: "The economy's not good, people aren't giving," or "I don't know anyone with money." These are perhaps the two most pervasive and persistent misconceptions about fundraising. The data presented in this exercise help to debunk these and several other myths.

Why Do This Exercise?
To reduce resistance to fundraising based on inaccurate information

Use This Exercise When
Your board and volunteers lack a basic understanding of philanthropy

Time Required
20 minutes

Audience
Anyone involved with your

fundraising campaign: some combination of board, staff, and volunteers

Setting
A space large enough to accommodate several small groups of three to five each

Materials
- Flip chart paper and markers
- Quiz form (page 39)

FACILITATING THE EXERCISE

This activity is structured as a quiz that participants discuss and complete in small groups. You'll need to photocopy the quiz (see page 39) in advance. The answers appear below.

1. Ask your colleagues to gather in groups of three to five to work on the quiz together.

2. Hand out copies of the quiz and give participants no more than ten minutes to discuss and complete it.

3. Reconvene the entire group and review each question, giving the correct answers.

4. Once you've reviewed all the answers, help the group draw conclusions. Use the following debriefing questions:

- What surprised you?
- What are the implications for our fundraising strategy? Do we need to think differently?

Emphasize that in fundraising, like many areas of life, we have a tendency to project our feelings and experiences onto others, even though our assumptions may not be accurate. For example, "I give money to my church and two others organizations; therefore, everyone else focuses their giving on a small number of nonprofits." In fact, most donors support a range of organizations, as noted in the quiz.

There are times when what we think we know is actually wrong. When it comes to fundraising, if the data trump personal experience, then we have to respect the data.

For example, your colleagues may perceive fundraising as competitive. When you show them that a typical household contributes to five to ten nonprofits per year, they may see it as less competitive, since most people who donate tend to spread their money around pretty broadly.

Answers appear below.

1. In a typical recent year, how much money did U.S. nonprofits raise from private philanthropy?
   a) $100 billion
   b) $200 billion
   c) **$300 billion**—the total varies somewhat year to year, but this is a good estimate
   d) $400 billion

2. Here are the four sources of private philanthropy. What percentage of total giving comes from each category? The total adds up to 100%.
a) Foundations	15%
b) Corporations	6%
c) Individuals	72%
d) Bequests	7%

3. Which nonprofit community raises the most money from private sources?
   a) Colleges and universities
   b) Health care
   c) **Religious organizations** receive about 32% of charitable giving
   d) Arts
   e) Social services/human services

4. How much do U.S. nonprofits receive from all sources: private giving, government funding, and fees and other earned income?
   a) $800 million
   b) $1 trillion
   c) $1.2 trillion
   d) **$1.5 trillion**—this amount equals roughly 10 percent of the U.S. economy

5. What percentage of American households donate to nonprofit organizations?
   a) 60%
   b) **70%**—some sources say 80%, so that would also be an acceptable answer
   c) 80%
   d) 90%

6. The typical American household supports how many charitable organizations per year?
   a) 1-2
   b) 3-4
   c) **5-10**
   d) More than 10

7. How much is median household giving per year?
   a) Less than $500
   b) $500-$1,000
   c) **$1,000-$2,000**
   d) More than $2,000

8. Which demographic group gives away the most money *as a percentage of household income*?
   a) **The poor**
   b) Middle income
   c) The wealthy

Sources: *Giving USA; National Center for Charitable Statistics; Nonprofit Quarterly; Grassroots Fundraising Journal*

TRAINING TIP When sharing the correct answers, use a little showmanship. For example, you can write the answers on a flip chart page in advance and fold the page in half, taping the bottom edge of the paper to the top of the easel. Then slide the edge down, revealing one answer at a time.

Where's The Money?

FUNDRAISING QUIZ

1. In a typical recent year, how much money did U.S. nonprofits raise from private philanthropy?
   - a) $100 billion
   - b) $200 billion
   - c) $300 billion
   - d) $400 billion

2. Here are the four sources of private philanthropy. What percentage of giving comes from each category? The total adds up to 100%.
   - a) Foundations
   - b) Corporations
   - c) Individuals
   - d) Bequests

3. Which nonprofit community raises the most money from private sources?
   - a) Colleges and universities
   - b) Health care
   - c) Religious organizations
   - d) Arts
   - e) Social services/human services

4. How much do U.S. nonprofits receive from all sources: private giving, government funding, and fees and other earned income?
   - a) $800 million
   - b) $1 trillion
   - c) $1.2 trillion
   - d) $1.5 trillion

5. What percentage of American households donate to nonprofit organizations?
   - a) 60%
   - b) 70%
   - c) 80%
   - d) 90%

6. The typical American household supports how many charitable organizations per year?
    a) 1-2
    b) 3-4
    c) 5-10
    d) More than 10

7. How much is median household giving per year?
    a) Less than $500
    b) $500-$1,000
    c) $1,000-$2,000
    d) More than $2,000

8. Which demographic group gives away the most money *as a percentage of household income*?
    a) The poor
    b) Middle income
    c) The wealthy

Sources: *Giving USA; National Center for Charitable Statistics; Nonprofit Quarterly; Grassroots Fundraising Journal*

Cycle of Fundraising

This exercise reduces resistance by helping people move past the idea that fundraising equals asking for money. You can create a menu of ways everyone—board, staff, volunteers, donors—can participate, even if they're unwilling to be askers. If you want to develop a fundraising culture throughout your organization, this is a great way to start.

Why Do This Exercise?
It's an easy first step to creating a model for strengthening relationships with your donors

Use This Exercise When
You want to emphasize that asking for gifts is only a small part of a larger process

Time Required
60 minutes

Audience
All participants in your fundraising campaign: some combination of board, staff, and volunteers

Setting
A space large enough to accommodate several small groups of three to five

Materials
- Flip chart paper and markers
- Three handouts: Cycle of Fundraising, North Lakeland Discovery Center Donor Engagement Menu, and Cycle of Fundraising: Building a Donor Engagement Menu (See pages 44-46)

FACILITATING THE EXERCISE

1. Photocopy the handouts in advance.

2. Share copies of the Cycle of Fundraising handout (page 44) with your trainees. Explain that this is a simple map for creating healthy, mutually beneficial relationships with donors. Note that only a fraction of the work is asking for money. Most of the cycle is about what happens before and after asking.

3. As a warm-up for the small group work to follow, ask the full group to brainstorm one or two activities that might fit into each phase. For example, "What are some of the ways we might identify prospective donors?" (Two possible answers: compile lists of friends, and review published donor lists from peer organizations.) Ask similar questions for each phase

of the donor cycle—"What steps could we take to educate and cultivate donors?"—encouraging an answer or two for each phase.

4. Once the large-group brainstorm is complete, distribute copies of the donor relationship menu developed by the North Lakeland Discovery Center (page 45). Explain that it was created by board and staff working together. Give participants a few moments to review the handout and ask questions.

5. Ask your colleagues to form small groups of three to five. Share copies of the worksheet Cycle of Fundraising: Building a Donor Engagement Menu (page 46). Ask each small group to fill it in, brainstorming one stage of the cycle at a time: "What are our different options for identifying prospects? Fill in the relevant box. How about educating and cultivating those prospects?" And so on. Let them know they will have about fifteen minutes to complete the worksheet.

6. While the small groups are brainstorming, write the following titles—one per sheet—on flip chart paper:

   • Identify Prospects
   • Educate, Cultivate, Involve
   • Ask
   • Thank and Recognize
   • Involve More Deeply

7. After about fifteen minutes, reconvene everyone into the large group to report their work. Begin by collecting all the items for Identify Prospects, writing them on the relevant flip chart page. Then collect the items for Educate, Cultivate, Involve. Capture all ideas for each stage in the cycle before moving to the next.

8. To debrief this exercise, use some combination of the following questions as you discuss each flip chart page:

   • Which of these tasks are we already doing?
   • What steps do we need to focus on to improve our donor relations?
   • Are there any specific tasks you would like to help with?

9. To conclude, draw a large circle on a piece of flip chart paper. With the help of the participants, divide the circle into a pie chart graph indicating how much time your organization should spend on each of the five functions. For an example, see page 47.

As you wrap up, ask for a volunteer to transcribe your flip chart notes into the Cycle of Fundraising template. It will provide a simple one-page map outlining your donor identification and engagement strategy. It also creates a menu of ways everyone in the organization can assist with fundraising, including many ways that don't involve asking.

TRAINING TIP Templates help people understand new concepts in a tangible way. While not necessary, we have found that reviewing a completed template (see next pages) helps people build a model that fits their own organizations. We have tried this exercise both ways—sharing the template first vs. allowing the group to build its own from scratch—and can vouch that using the template early in the exercise is very helpful.

Cycle of Fundraising

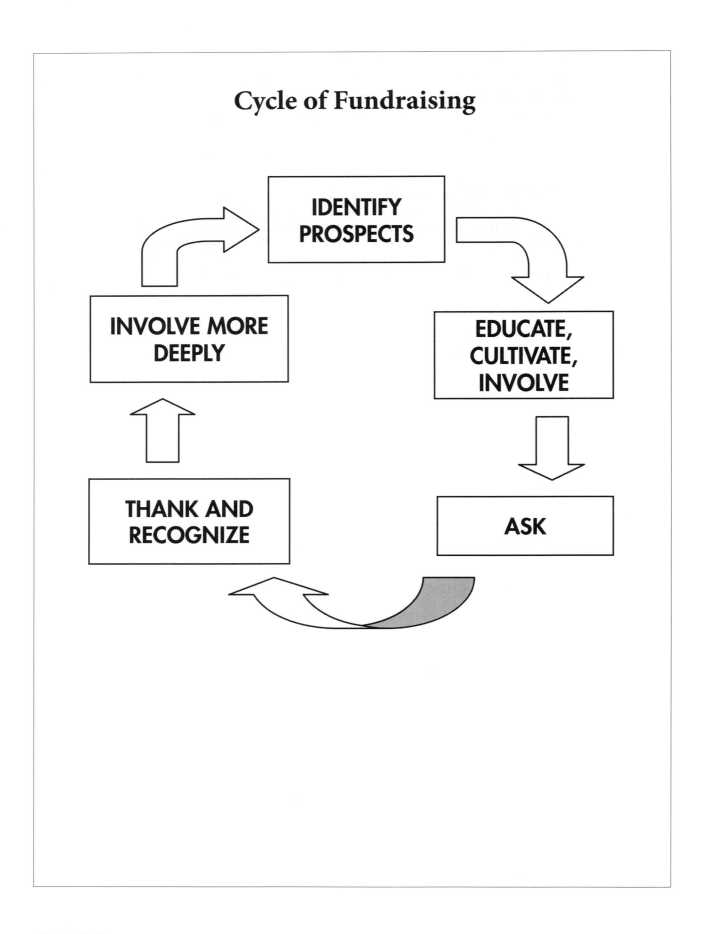

North Lakeland
Discovery Center

Cycle of Development: Expanding Your Connection

Naturally Inspiring and Enriching Lives through Meaningful Connections with Nature, People and Community

www.DiscoveryCenter.net • (877) 543-2085 • Contact@DiscoveryCenter.net

Identify Prospects

1. EAD and Staff identify potential foundation grants.
2. Seek and refer board members with fundraising experience.
3. Actively seek potential donors/volunteers.
4. Review donor lists for potential donors who have given to similar organizations.
5. Have a designated person(s) to talk to referrals.

Inclusive Involvement

1. Train volunteer-donors to give Center tours
2. Ask donors to assist, lead or invite them to programs and events.
3. Invite donors to join Board, committees or focus groups.
4. Ask donors to write a story for newsletter on personal importance of DC.
5. Ask donors to host house parties in concert with board members, and to make intro/open doors.
6. Ask donors for feedback on planning, fundraising, and other organization-wide initiatives.

Educate and Cultivate

1. Develop the why through an "elevator speech". Train staff and board.
2. Host donor dinners and events with time dedicated to the DC story.
3. Tours—train ambassadors on "elevator speech."
4. Ask donors to talk to donors, and provide opportunities for roundtable discussions.
5. Create Q&A with common questions, and include how to learn about upcoming events, who to call to be involved.
6. Articles and photos in newsletters (e.g., bequests, memorial gifts; personal stories from participants).
7. Seek out media attention for grant receipts and DC story-telling opportunities.

The System: A volunteer and donor tracking database is key to providing personalized attention and to communicating respectfully.

Thank and Recognize

1. Board makes quarterly calls to new donors $250+.
2. Informal thank you's (e.g., at event or program).
3. Invite and recognize sponsors, item donors and volunteers at summer recognition events.
4. Host Voyageur Dinner and Member Appreciation Night/Annual Meeting.
5. Publicize names of supporters in annual flier and otherwise as appropriate.
6. Send donors CDs, DVDs and other visual gifts thanking them.
7. Personalize gifts and notes.
8. Encourage attendees at events to patronize supporters and sponsors – and frequent their establishments yourselves.

The Ask

1. Face to face visits (collaborative)
2. At house parties and other events as appropriate.
3. Website, email and social media asks.
4. Letters (e.g., sponsor) and follow up calls.
5. Identify challenge or matching donor gifts.
6. Make calls supporting a special event.
7. Solicit/give items for silent or live auctions.
8. Recruit new members.

Cycle of Fundraising

BUILDING A DONOR ENGAGEMENT MENU

Create a menu of activities for each stage of the relationship:

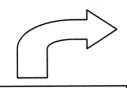

Identify Prospects

1.
2.
3.
4.
5.
6.

Involve More Deeply

1.
2.
3.
4.
5.
6.

Educate, Cultivate, Involve

1.
2.
3.
4.
5.
6.

Thank and Recognize

1.
2.
3.
4.
5.
6.

The Ask

1.
2.
3.
4.
5.
6.

Cycle of Fundraising Time Allocation

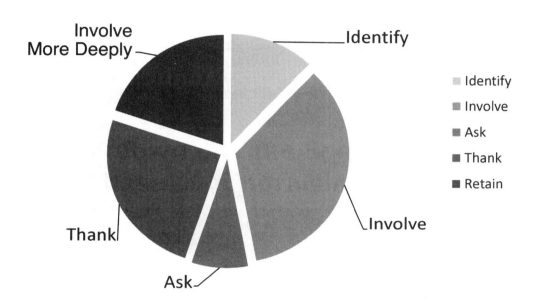

Breakdown of Time Spent on Each Phase of Fundraising Cycle

- Identify
- Involve
- Ask
- Thank
- Retain

Involve More Deeply — Identify — Involve — Ask — Thank

Adapted from Tina Cincotti, Funding Change Consulting.
Used with permission. Thanks, Tina!

Fundraising on Faith

 00:15

By presenting a familiar model, this exercise reminds people they already know more about fundraising than they realize. Those of us raising money for secular organizations would be wise to study the techniques and attitudes of faith communities, because in many ways they are role models. Rather than relying solely on divine inspiration, many intentionally build a culture of fundraising throughout their congregations. Even the "unchurched" will be familiar enough with faith fundraising models to participate in this activity.

Why Do This Exercise?
We are surrounded by fundraising role models—let's learn from their experience

Use This Exercise When
You want people to see how fundraising is a part of everyday life

Time Required
15 minutes

Audience
Anyone involved with your fundraising campaign: some combination of board, staff, and volunteers

Setting
A space large enough to accommodate several small groups of three to five

Materials
Flip chart paper and markers

FACILITATING THE EXERCISE

1. Point out that year after year, one-third of all charitable dollars are given to faith-based organizations: churches, synagogues, mosques, temples, ashrams, and other faith communities.

2. Ask your colleagues to form small groups of three to five to discuss and answer the following question: Why are faith organizations so successful at raising money?

3. After five to ten minutes, reconvene the large group to collect their responses, which you can write on the flip chart. Among the likely answers:

    -   **They ask.** And ask. And ask. Many pass the basket every week—even multiple times a week.

    -   **They ask everybody.** Faith-based organizations make little distinction between the rich and the poor. No one is screened in or out due to their *assumed* ability, or lack of ability, to give.

- **They ask for large amounts.** In the Christian tradition, it's a tithe: 10 percent of income. (Do you have the courage to ask *your* donors for 10 percent of their incomes?)

- **It's expected.** There is little shame or guilt regarding "the ask." Indeed, it's accepted that everybody who attends is a donor or potential donor who would benefit from giving.

- **They provide lots of options.** In addition to the weekly gifts solicited by some denominations, most houses of worship request an annual donation from their members. Then there's the building fund, overseas relief fund, social justice fund, youth development fund—you get the idea. Everyone is expected to give, but donors have a choice in how they direct their gifts.

- **Volunteers ask for the gifts.** Most church fundraising is built on the work of volunteers who not only pass the basket but also lead the annual canvass of the congregation and organize fundraising events. The highest form of fundraising is peer to peer—that is, one donor soliciting another—and faith-based groups have perfected this model.

- **They do a great job building relationships.** Faith institutions see their constituents several times per month: at worship services, family programs, religious study, leadership meetings, and community action projects. They know their people really, really well. When it's time to ask for gifts, these relationships pay off.

4. Debrief the exercise by asking the following questions:

- For those who are involved with a religious organization, how has faith-based fundraising affected your approach to giving?
- What can our organization learn from faith-based fundraising that would improve our results?
- How can we build deeper, more meaningful relationships with our donors and supporters?

TRAINING TIP This is a great opportunity for storytelling, since many people raised in religious households will talk about giving behavior in their families and congregations. Encourage your colleagues to tell these stories. With few exceptions, they will reinforce the messages you're trying to convey through this activity.

Fundraising Effectiveness Quiz

 00:20

We could have written a book about fundraising strategies that feel easy and safe—email, anyone?—but are basically inefficient. Instead, we've chosen to focus on the most effective way to raise money: face to face. Unfortunately, this is also the scariest. One of the first steps in addressing this fear is to help your trainees compare various fundraising strategies. Otherwise you may never escape the treadmill of impersonal mail appeals or multiple fundraising events that leave everyone exhausted.

Why Do This Exercise?
To help everyone understand that personal asking is the most effective strategy

Use This Exercise When
Every fundraising suggestion from your board is about adding more benefit events

Time Required
20 minutes

Audience
Anyone involved with your fundraising campaign: some combination of board, staff, and volunteers

Setting
A space large enough to accommodate several small groups of three to five

Materials
- Flip chart paper and markers
- Fundraising effectiveness quiz (see page 53)

FACILITATING THE EXERCISE

1. This activity is structured as a quiz that people discuss and complete in small groups. You will need to photocopy the quiz (see page 53) in advance. The answers appear below.

2. Ask your colleagues to gather in groups of three to five to work on the quiz together.

3. Hand out the quiz and ask participants to discuss the strategies and rank them 1 through 10, with 1 being the most effective. Encourage them to think about which approaches generate the most money for the time,

effort, and cost invested. Give participants no more than ten minutes to discuss the questions and decide on the answers.

4. Reconvene the full group and reveal the answers. For those who are skeptical, explain that these data are drawn from the research of the Fundraising School at the Center for Philanthropy at Indiana University, the leading U.S. academic center studying fundraising and giving. It's helpful to know and respect the data, even when (especially when) they contradict our personal beliefs and experience. Fundraising is equal parts science and art, and we ignore the science at our peril.

5. Debrief the exercise by asking the following questions:

   • What surprised you? Why?
   • What are the advantages of pairing up to meet with donors?

   Answers to why two donors are better than one might include more courage, more wisdom, and the hope that at least one person (in some cases, a board member or volunteer) has a strong relationship with the donor but may not be willing to ask for the gift. Think about this person as the "door opener." Bonus points for the following answers: deeper listening potential with two solicitors and a greater chance of long-term continuity with the donor. If only one person knows the donor and that person leaves your organization, you may have to rebuild the relationship from scratch.

   • Why are benefit events ranked so low?

   To facilitate this topic, draw a vertical line down the center of a flip chart sheet. Put a plus mark (+) on one side of the page and a minus mark (-) on the other side. Ask everyone to brainstorm the pros and cons of fundraising events. You will likely fill the page with a robust list of both pros and cons. The message: if you choose to organize fundraising events, make sure that everyone understands both the risks and opportunities and also acknowledges that time and energy you devote to events aren't available for other (generally more efficient) strategies. Economists call this the "opportunity cost" of choosing one strategy over another.

   • How can we do more to focus our efforts on the most effective strategies?

ANSWERS

1. Face-to-face request with a team of two askers
2. Face-to-face request with one asker
3. Personal letter on personal stationery; telephone follow-up will improve results
4. Personal phone call; follow-up letter will improve results
    (NOTE: Inverting 3 and 4 would still count as a correct answer, since this can vary by the age of the donor.)
5. Personalized letter (hand-signed with note) or personalized email
6. Impersonal form letter (direct mail) or impersonal email
7. Impersonal telephone (telemarketing)
8. Fundraising benefit/special event
9. Door-to-door canvassing
10. Media, traditional and social/advertising/Internet

This exercise used with permission of The Fund Raising School at the Center on Philanthropy at Indiana University.

TRAINING TIP Encourage cheering and booing while you give the answers. If people have correctly answered the question and want to celebrate, that's great. You could even hand out noisemakers. And if your trainees disagree with the answer and want to express their unhappiness, why not? A little lusty booing makes any workshop more lively.

Fundraising Effectiveness Quiz

_____ Impersonal telephone call (telemarketing)

_____ Fundraising benefit/special event

_____ Face-to-face request with a team of two askers

_____ Impersonal form letter (direct mail)/impersonal email

_____ Media, traditional and social/advertising/Internet

_____ Personal letter on personal stationery

_____ Door-to-door canvassing (with paid canvassers)

_____ Personalized form letter (hand-signed with note) or personalized email

_____ Face-to-face request with one asker

_____ Personal telephone call

Used with permission of The Fund Raising School at the Center on Philanthropy at Indiana University.

If Money Wasn't Scarce 🏛 📐 📝 00:45

When Andy worked as a development director, he would gather the program staff once a year to ask the "what if" questions: What if we had all the money we needed? What if we could do the work we wanted without worrying about the budget—what would we do? What if we had the capacity to try new things and do our work differently, what would that look like?

The resulting brainstorm was beneficial in several ways. First, it generated interesting program ideas, some of which came to fruition. Second, it provided an opportunity to talk about "fundability" as a filter for evaluating these options—in other words, whether and why an idea is likely to attract grants and donations. Perhaps most important, it shifted the collective thinking—at least momentarily—from scarcity to abundance.

All successful fundraising begins with an attitude of abundance: the money is out there; let's get organized and raise it.

Why Do This Exercise? To help your organization move past the "scarcity mentality"	**Audience** Primarily staff, though board leadership might also benefit from participating
Use This Exercise When You're creating a strategic plan or annual work plan, or simply to help your colleagues think more broadly about what's possible	**Setting** Anywhere you gather to work on your campaign plan and train your participants
Time Required 30-45 minutes	**Materials** • Flip chart paper and markers • Paper and pens

FACILITATING THE EXERCISE

1. Gather your coworkers around a table or in a circle and ask the following questions: "If we had all the money we needed, how would our work change? What would we be doing that we aren't doing now?"

   If you have five or fewer coworkers, brainstorm with the full group. With six or more, create smaller breakout groups of at least three participants. Allow fifteen to twenty minutes for this conversation.

2. If you're working with one large group, write any ideas on the flip chart paper as they are discussed. With breakouts, reconvene everyone and ask for reports from each group, writing their ideas on the flip chart as they're presented.

3. To debrief this exercise, ask the following questions:

    -   What did this brainstorm feel like?
    -   Which of these ideas seems most fundable to you? Why?
    -   Do we want to test these ideas with any other audience? How about our board? Our constituents? Our funders?

4. If you decide to share your thinking with others, work with the group to make assignments (who will talk with whom) and set a deadline for completing the task.

TRAINING TIP The concept of fundability is imprecise—it's more intuitive than measurable. Fundability includes some combination of a clear need, timeliness or urgency, creative problem solving, capacity to deliver, and a strong "hook." Hooks can be emotional—for example, a compelling story—or perhaps a new way of framing and addressing a longstanding problem. Seasoned fundraisers develop a strong sense of which programs and initiatives have sales appeal and which don't.

As a facilitator, you don't need to be an expert on fundability. Your job is to tease out the reasons why people believe a particular idea has the potential—or not—to attract funding. Testing your ideas with others (see step 4 above) will help to clarify which ones might have traction.

PART 3

Making the Case

We seldom talk anyone into anything. Usually, people talk themselves into doing what they want to do, and making a gift is no exception. As a fundraiser, your job is more about listening than trying to convince someone to give. Still, sooner or later solicitors must make the case for your organization. When they know why they're asking and what they're asking for, they'll feel less anxious and more excited about discussing the cause.

The best cases are all about passion and caring. They don't emphasize what an organization needs but rather what it will accomplish. They look forward rather than backward. And they are BRIEF—often as brief as a few minutes.

Before we dive into these case-building exercises, a cautionary tale. A wealthy friend was visited by three people from a large, well-respected college. Their expressed goal: to ask for a large gift. As a former trustee, our friend knew a lot about the school and expected a lively conversation. That's not what happened.

The three experienced solicitors—the president, development director, and a board member—sat down and after a bit of chitchat, began to make the case. First the president spoke about the college. Then the development director spoke about the fundraising campaign. Finally the board member chimed in with a request for $250,000.

By the time they stopped talking, forty-five minutes had passed and our friend hadn't spoken a word.

These three well-meaning people—all experienced fundraisers and excited about making the case—had forgotten the critical element in face-to-face fundraising: opening the door to a meaningful conversation. They could have described the fundraising campaign in a minute or two and then asked the donor to share her thoughts on the college, the case, and the campaign. But that's not what they did. And when our friend told us about it, she related with chilling simplicity how disrespected she felt.

As you lead your colleagues through these exercises, stress that an effective solicitor makes a very (!) brief case, then initiates a substantive conversation that helps donors do what's right for them.

What Drew You to This Work?

 00:15

Many boards and committees are all business and devote little time to discussing the personal and emotional aspects of an organization and its work. Nobody ever joined a board or volunteered for a nonprofit because they loved going to meetings, talking about policies and procedures, or looking at spreadsheets. They join because they want to make a difference in the world.

As a fundraiser, your greatest asset is your enthusiasm for the mission and work of your organization, so it's helpful to remind yourself why you care. This exercise can generate useful language for building your case and talking with donors.

Why Do This Exercise?
It reduces fundraising to its elemental level: two people talking about something they both care about

Use This Exercise When
You want your board members and volunteers to know one another better and understand their motivations for serving on the board

Time Required
10-15 minutes

Audience
Anyone involved with your fundraising campaign: some combination of board, staff, and volunteers

Setting
A quiet space large enough for people to pair up, talk, and hear each other

Materials
Flip chart paper and markers (optional)

FACILITATING THE EXERCISE

1. Ask people to pair up, preferably with someone they don't know well.

2. Instruct the partners to ask each other the following questions:

   - Why are you involved with this organization?
   - Why is our work important to you?
   - Tell me about a time when you saw our mission in action and what it meant to you.

Encourage partners to add whatever follow-up questions are needed to flesh out the answers. Such a follow-up might be "Can you tell me a specific story or example about your involvement with our work?"

3. Give the pairs five to seven minutes to complete this task. Part-way through, you might warn them, "You've got another two minutes, so if you haven't told your own story yet, please do so now."

4. Reconvene the full group. Debrief the exercise with the following questions:

    - What was the most memorable thing you heard from your partner?
    - What did you learn about our organization?
    - As we're discussing this, what common themes are you hearing?

    If you like, you can write key phrases on the flip chart.

5. Conclude the exercise by summarizing the range of reasons why people choose to be involved. Skilled solicitors are always listening for the link between the work of the organization and each individual donor's interests, passions, and experiences.

TRAINING TIP Writing ideas or comments from the participants lets them know that they've been heard and that they're doing valuable work. If you choose to paraphrase, check with the speaker first and ask permission before changing the words: "May I write that as ...?"

What's Our Mission?

 00:15

When it comes to outreach, marketing, and fundraising, it's helpful to have your leaders delivering the same message in their own words. This exercise helps them learn—from each other—the most compelling ways to describe the work of your organization.

Why Do This Exercise?
Because your board members may not be clear or articulate about what your organization actually does

Use This Exercise When
You want everyone to talk about your mission in ways that are comfortable, personal, and accurate

Time Required
15 minutes

Audience
Your board

Setting
Your meeting room or any room with a table large enough to accommodate all board members

Materials
Paper and pens

FACILITATING THE EXERCISE

1. Seat the board members around a table with blank paper and pens. Remove all other materials (e.g., board notebooks) from the table.

2. Let everyone know this exercise isn't a quiz and there is no "right answer." The goal is to hear participants talk about the organization and its work in their own words, rather than see if they can remember the formal mission statement or "elevator speech."

3. Ask each board member to write, in his or her own words, the mission of the organization.

4. When finished, go around the table and ask each board member to read what he or she has written, one by one.

5. To debrief this first round, ask people to discuss the following questions:

   • What were the most memorable phrases you heard?

- Did you hear anything that appealed to your emotions? If so, what was it?
- Did you hear any discordant notes? Are we all in agreement, more or less?

6. Collect the papers. Then go around the table a second time—this time, in the opposite direction—and ask everyone to describe the mission in their own words without writing or reading anything.

7. To debrief the second round, ask the following questions:

- Did you hear anything you want to borrow and use yourself?
- When you're talking to friends about our work, what if anything will you say differently as a result of this conversation?

TRAINING TIP If any of your colleagues are totally off message or simply don't understand the mission, be supportive. "Jane, that's an interesting take on what we do. It's a bit different from what I heard from the others. Can you say a little more about how that connects to our mission?" Depending on the answer, you might quietly identify someone to privately coach Jane after the meeting.

Features and Benefits: What Are We Selling?

Do you know the difference between a feature and a benefit? This distinction is the heart of marketing theory. Simply put, you describe something by listing its features, and you sell it by recounting what it can do: its benefits. A drill, for example, might include a sixteenth-inch drill bit. That's a feature. But people buy it because of the hole it can drill, rather than the bit or even the drill itself. Yes, the hole is the benefit.

In this exercise, we apply the distinction between features and benefits to fundraising. It will help board and staff members identify the most powerful reasons for supporting your organization and become more confident in discussing your organization with others.

Why Do This Exercise?
Because one of the great mistakes in fundraising is selling the features rather than the benefits

Use This Exercise When
You are working to develop compelling messages for your organization

Time Required
20 minutes

Audience
Your board, staff, or any committee that serves the organization

Setting
Anywhere you gather to work on your campaign plan and train your participants

Materials
- Two easels with flip chart paper and markers
- A fork or other common object

FACILITATING THE EXERCISE

This exercise includes two parts. The first uses an everyday object - we sometimes use a fork - to clarify the distinction between features and benefits. The second part applies that distinction to your organization.

1. Prepare two flip chart pages for each section. Put the word FEATURES on the top of one page and the word BENEFITS on the other.

2. Hold up the object you have selected and ask people to identify its features. If you use a fork, features will include four tines, made of metal or plastic,

approximately five inches long, curved handle, decorative markings, and the like. The point is that features describe the fork.

3. Then ask for a list of benefits, i.e, what the fork can accomplish. The list might include getting food to your mouth, keeping your hands clean, minimizing the spread of germs, enabling you to handle hot food.

4. Once you have a reasonable list of features and benefits, turn the flip chart pages and again write FEATURES on the top of one and BENEFITS on the other.

5. Now ask everyone first to itemize the features of your organization and then its benefits. Remember that your buildings, staff, committees, and financial management systems are all features, but the results of your work in the community are benefits.

6. Once you've completed these lists—don't let this drag on—ask your colleagues how they might use the benefits to describe your organization. For example, if you provide food to hungry children, one benefit is that kids do better in school when they're well fed. If you work to protect wild lands in your local watershed, one benefit is clean drinking water which also saves taxpayer money by not having to build a new filtration plant.

7. To debrief the exercise, ask the following questions:

   • Which benefits should we highlight to describe our organization?
   • In our current materials, do we focus on features or benefits?
   • How might we strengthen the ways we talk about our organization?

By completing the exercise, you can shift donor conversations from features to benefits, which is a far more powerful and productive approach. Rather than describing the physical features of your building, you can talk about how that building makes it possible for you to care for your clients: "In our new building, we provide a full range of free health care services to all patients, including those who are disabled."

We thank our colleague Michael Miller for sharing this exercise.

TRAINING TIP When you introduce an exercise, let people know at the start how much time it will take. That gives you leverage to move the discussion along and wrap it up efficiently. If someone is talking too long, thank them for their thoughts but call attention to the time remaining.

Destination Postcard

 `00:15`

What would success look like for your organization? If you saw it—literally saw it—would you recognize it? This simple exercise will help your board and staff members visualize success and create the language to describe it.

Why Do This Exercise?
A vision of success—the more tangible, the better—inspires people to do their best work

Use This Exercise When
You're starting a new organization or a new program, or you are so mired in the details of ongoing work that the "big picture" has become obscured

Time Required
15 minutes

Audience
Anyone involved with your fundraising campaign: some combination of board, staff, and volunteers

Setting
A room large enough to accommodate everyone around one table or a circle of chairs

Materials
- Blank postcards (not picture postcards)
- Stamps (optional)

FACILITATING THE EXERCISE

1. Hand out the postcards and give the following instructions: "Imagine after a long journey you've arrived at a destination, and that destination is what our community (our country, our world) will look like when our organization's work is complete. Write a postcard to a friend describing what you're experiencing—what you see and hear, how it feels, and so forth. Make it conversational, but remember: it has to fit on a postcard."

2. After a few minutes, go around the circle and ask everyone to read what they've written.

3. To debrief this exercise, pose the following questions:

    - What was your experience writing the postcard? What did it feel like to think about our organization's success?
    - When you listened to people reading their cards, what did you notice? Were there any common themes? Did you hear any common language?
    - How might this exercise change the way we think about and talk about our work?

4. As an optional wrap-up, write the names of everyone present on slips of paper, put them in a basket, and ask participants to draw a name. Then ask them to address their postcard to the name they drew. Collect the cards, add stamps, wait a few days, and mail them.

When the postcard arrives in the mail, it will remind people of their experience in this exercise and of your organization's goals. If people draw their own names, so be it—sometimes it's helpful to send *yourself* a message.

We thank our colleague Ma'ayan Simon of Converge Here for sharing this exercise.

TRAINING TIP While you may feel inspired to use picture postcards for this activity, blank postcards allow more room to write.

Making Headlines

 00:45

There's a certain magic that comes with articulating a vision of what could be. This exercise will push your leaders to envision what your community (or the world) might look like if your organization solved the problems it addresses. By focusing on a vision of the future, you can expand your collective imagination and shift your thinking from short-term, practical steps to long-range. aspirational accomplishments. In doing so, you'll help connect everyone with the real reasons you do the work you do.

Why Do This Exercise?
To keep sight of why you do the work you do, which often gets lost among mundane challenges

Use This Exercise When
You want to inspire people to think in a more expansive way about the potential of your organization

Time Required
30-45 minutes, depending on the size of the group. The more small groups you create, the longer it will take

Audience
Your board or any other development committee. This exercise works best with twelve or more participants, so you can organize them into four groups

Setting
A space large enough to accommodate several small groups of three to five

Materials
- One flip chart page for each group, with markers
- Tape (unless you're using self-stick flip chart paper)

FACILITATING THE EXERCISE

1. Begin by asking participants to imagine that five years from now, they are reading an article about one of your organization's most important programs. The article reflects the tremendous accomplishments of your work and the resulting change in your community.

2. Ask each person to take two minutes to write a headline for the imagined article that reflects the accomplishment but DOES NOT mention the name of your organization. Here's an example: "Teen Pregnancy Rate Cut in Half in Mott Haven Neighborhood; Girls' Graduation Rate Also Dramatically Up."

3. Assemble the participants into small groups of three to five. Ask members of each group to share their headlines among themselves. Then have them select the most exciting one, write it on a flip chart page, and post it on the wall so everyone can easily read it. This works best if you post all the headlines side by side.

4. Ask someone from each table to read the headline from their group.

5. After all the headlines are posted and read, debrief using the following questions with the full group:

   - What makes these headlines powerful? Feel free to move down the line, pointing out any that work especially well and asking the group to discuss why.
   - How might we craft the case for our organization so it's as strong as these headlines? For example, can we talk about our work simply and emotionally without using jargon or technical language? Can we highlight the difference we make in the community rather than our programs?
   - If we created headlines that focused on our *donors*—in addition to focusing on our community impact—what would those headlines say? For example, "Neighbors donate money and time—homeless family gets a home." This is important because it honors the essential role of donors and volunteers and thereby makes them central to the story of your success.

Conclude the discussion by reminding the group that an effective case for giving is a primary fundraising tool. Painting a vision based on solutions is one way to strengthen your case and give it greater impact.

We thank our colleague Michael Miller for sharing this exercise.

TRAINING TIP When dividing a group into subgroups, the count-off method works nicely. If you have a group of 15 people and you want five groups of three, ask people to count off 1, 2, 3, 4, 5 ... 1, 2, 3, 4, 5 ... 1, 2, 3, 4, 5 until everyone has a number. Then instruct the 1s to form a group, the 2s to form a group, and so forth. This approach "shuffles the deck" and creates a mix of people who may have been sitting in different parts of the room.

The Case, Simplified

For those who don't know what to say to a donor, this exercise offers a quick and easy way to outline a fundraising pitch. It reinforces the idea that your staff and volunteer leaders already know enough about your work to go out and raise money.

Why Do This Exercise?
To reduce some of the mystery about how to talk with donors

Use This Exercise When
You want a fun, thoughtful activity that engages people and makes them feel knowledgeable

Time Required
30-45 minutes

Audience
All participants in your fundraising campaign: some combination of board, staff, and volunteers

Setting
Anywhere you gather to work on your campaign plan and train your participants

Materials
- Stopwatch or timer
- Bell or whistle (optional)
- The Case, Simplified — Worksheet (page 69)

FACILITATING THE EXERCISE

1. Photocopy the worksheet on page 69 in advance.

2. Hand out copies of the worksheet with the following instructions: "Please write your name on the top of the page. We're going to fill in this form one question at a time and do it quickly—so please don't work ahead. Write as legibly as you can. First question: What are we proud of about our organization? Write down three things you're most proud of. You've got one minute for this question. Go!"

3. After one minute—give them a little more time, if needed—ring the bell. Ask for volunteers to read one or two items on their list; keep doing this until you've heard several of the items.

4. Read question two with the same instructions: "You've got one minute. Go!"

5. Continue this process through the final question, giving participants two minutes to make notes about their favorite anecdotes. Once they're done, recruit two or three volunteers to tell their favorite stories. You can also ask for feedback: "What made that story effective? How could the storyteller improve it?"

6. Debrief this exercise with the following questions:

   - What was your experience filling in the form? Did you find it easy? Challenging? Why?
   - When we discussed our answers, did you hear any that really stuck with you? Which ones? Why?

7. As you complete the exercise, make the following point: "Each of you just wrote a fundraising pitch, because when we're talking to donors, these are the things we talk about: What makes us proud of our work? What makes our work unique? Who are we trying to involve and engage? And finally: What's the story that sums it all up, that creates the emotional connection?"

8. Collect the worksheets and recruit someone to compile and edit them. When this task is complete, you will have a great two-page summary any solicitor could use during the practice exercises in Chapter 6 or with an actual donor. Thinking more broadly, this case material is also useful for fundraising letters, email appeals, grant proposals, and so on.

TRAINING TIP As with any timed exercise, follow your instincts about how flexible to be on the timing. How many of your colleagues continue writing after one minute? How many are sitting around looking bored? Pay attention to their body language and adjust the time accordingly. As a general rule, it's better to move things along rather than let the exercise drag.

The Case, Simplified

WORKSHEET

What are we proud of? What's our impact in the community?
Write down three things about our organization that you're most proud of:

1. _____

2. _____

3. _____

Differentiation: What distinguishes us from other organizations?
What do we *have* or *do* that no one else has or does? It's okay to think about this geographically: "We are the only group in Washington County that …"

1. _____

2. _____

3. _____

Market segmentation: Who are we trying to reach?
List the audiences we want to reach for any purpose: education, service delivery, fundraising, advocacy, collaboration, and the like.

1. _____

2. _____

3. _____

4. _____

5. _____

What's your favorite story?
Write notes about your favorite anecdote or example that describes the impact of our work. Remember, "Statistics raise eyebrows but emotions raise money"—so go easy on the data and jargon. Pretend you're talking to a friend or neighbor.

_____

_____

_____

_____

One Minute of Fame

There's nothing like practice to help board members and volunteers talk comfortably and powerfully about your work. As an added benefit, they can be inspired by one another as they discover the words and phrases that work best for them. Along the way, they'll get to know each other a little better and strengthen their commitment to your organization.

This is an excellent follow-up to the Features and Benefits exercise on page 61. You can combine them at the same meeting, or conduct Features and Benefits first and this one later. This activity works well by itself, but be sure to review the material on features and benefits so you can summarize it easily.

Why Do This Exercise?
The most effective form of marketing is word of mouth, yet many people fear public speaking. If your board and staff can't or won't speak on your behalf, you'll miss many marketing opportunities

Use This Exercise When
Your colleagues need to find the right words to speak about your organization with passion and precision

Time Required
If you're disciplined, about 45 minutes for up to 15 people, but it could take longer with a larger group

Audience
Anyone involved in your fundraising campaign: some combination of board, staff, and volunteers

Setting
A space large enough to accommodate groups of three to five either at small tables or in clusters of chairs

Materials
• Stopwatch or timer
• Bell or whistle
• Paper and pens

FACILITATING THE EXERCISE

1. Organize the participants into groups of three to five. Ideally, you want at least three small groups. Ask everyone to imagine they've been asked to give a one-minute presentation to their service club, church group, alumni association, or other community organization.

   Remind them that the most powerful statements focus on benefits rather than features. Be prepared to explain the difference (see pages 61).

2. Give everyone three minutes to write an outline of their mini-speech. Once they're done, ask everyone to present their speeches, one after another, to their small group. (Each group will be doing this at the same time, so there'll be a buzz in the room.) Encourage them not to read from their notes, but rather to look at their colleagues while talking.

3. Time these speeches; after one minute use your bell or whistle to let the groups know it's time for the next speaker: "Speaker number two, get ready. Begin now!" This process continues with each subsequent speaker until each small group has heard from everyone in their group.

4. Once everyone has spoken, ask each group to select the speech they found most compelling and discuss what made it so.

5. After three or four minutes of discussion, have them repeat the exercise with everyone giving updated versions of their speeches. Give everyone a minute or so to make notes before the speeches begin. As before, time these rounds, using your bell or whistle to stop one speaker and start the next.

6. After the second round, ask each small group to select the most compelling speech to present to the full group.

7. Reconvene the full group to hear the speeches. Be sure to lead applause for each speaker.

8. Debrief this exercise using the following questions:

   • What did the most effective speeches have in common?
   • Were there specific words or phrases that jumped out at you? Why?
   • Which did you find more compelling—facts or stories? Why?

If there's no time for a full discussion, as an alternative you can ask the group to write down two things they want to use when they talk about the organization. Then quickly ask each person to read one of their items.

This exercise can be repeated throughout the year—for example, at subsequent board meetings. Over time, you will see your board members relax as they learn to speak with greater clarity, authority, and emotional impact.

TRAINING TIP We learn a lot through practice, but practicing in front of a large group can make people nervous. Using small groups reduces anxiety and helps people focus.

Six-Word Stories

Ernest Hemingway is said to have written the most famous six-word story: "For sale: baby shoes. Never worn." Indeed, these six words tell a sad tale succinctly and powerfully.

It's not easy to write a great six-word story but given a few minutes most people can come up with a pretty good one. Off the top of our heads, here's an example: "Learned how to ask. Watch out!" Or how about "Wanted: Fundraising chairman. Ours won't ask."

Why Do This Exercise?
Fundraising is storytelling—make every word count

Use This Exercise When
You want to end a meeting or training session on a note of creativity

Time Required
If you're disciplined, about 20 minutes

Audience
All participants in your fundraising campaign: some combination of board, staff, and volunteers

Setting
A room with enough wall or window space to post several sheets of flip chart paper

Materials
- Flip chart paper and markers
- Paper and pens
- Tape (unless you're using self-stick flip chart paper)

FACILITATING THE EXERCISE

1. Ask if anyone has ever heard a six-word story. Write Hemingway's famous example—"For sale: baby shoes. Never worn."—on a flip chart. Ask for opinions about what makes it effective.

2. Hand out a piece of paper to everyone and ask the group to write a six-word story about why your organization matters. Give them no more than two minutes.

3. While they're writing, post a few pages of flip chart paper on the wall. Post enough sheets so that everyone can write their stories; assume each page will include three or four stories.

4. As people finish, ask them come to the front of the room, take a marker, write their story, and return to their seats.

5. Once all the stories are written, ask each person to read his or hers, going around the room or the table in order.

6. To debrief this exercise, ask the following questions:

    - Which stories appealed to you? Why?
    - What did the most effective stories have in common?
    - Do these stories reveal any message we might use in our donor communications?

7. Collect the stories and recruit someone to compile and distribute them to the participants as a follow-up to the exercise.

We thank our colleague Paula Peter of The Solstice Group for sharing this exercise.

TRAINING TIP Novice trainers sometimes worry their group won't rise to the challenges offered by these exercises. But almost without exception, the people you train will be creative and smart beyond your expectations. As long as you provide the context for the exercise, clear instructions, and the right amount of time (sometimes less time is better than more), a group can accomplish great objectives.

PART 4

Building Blocks for Success

When you boil it down, two primary barriers stand in the way of successful fundraising: fear and poor systems. In previous chapters (especially chapter 1), we offer exercises to reduce the fear of fundraising. In this chapter, we want to help you improve your structure and systems.

These two barriers are often combined. People who fear fundraising will bring up all sorts of structural concerns to avoid asking for money: I don't understand the campaign calendar; we need better materials; I don't know enough about my prospects; when are we going to be trained? the database isn't giving us all the information; I need a fact sheet so I can answer any questions people might ask. And on and on.

While these may be legitimate concerns and requests, they generally mask the real issue: anxiety about asking. Even the most enthusiastic and inspired board members can get mired in their own anxiety without a clear, step-by-step plan with specific assignments, messages, and deadlines.

Good structure reduces stress. To help your board and staff raise money effectively, you need to help them decide who does what, when they do it, and with whom. What's your goal and how do you reach it?

Engage your volunteers and staff in answering these questions. It's one thing to go to a board meeting and present a fundraising plan you developed and hand out assignments. It's quite another to have your board help develop the plan. The greater their input, the deeper their understanding—and the more likely they'll follow through and implement the plan.

The exercises in this chapter will help your board and colleagues figure out how they can personally participate, how much money they want to raise, their collective goal for board giving, and the structure and timetable of the fundraising process.

Building a Board Fundraising Ladder

This activity is designed to generate a long list of board fundraising opportunities. When it's over, you'll have a rough step-by-step plan for increasing board engagement that you can refine as you go along.

Why Do This Exercise?
Everyone can find a fundraising role, even (especially) those who find fundraising scary or distasteful

Use This Exercise When
You're trying to alter the "culture of fundraising" on your board to make it more comprehensive and inclusive

Time Required
About 30 minutes, plus 10 minutes for preparation

Audience
The leadership team for your fundraising campaign: some combination of board, staff, and volunteers. This activity can be done with as few as three people and as many as a dozen. In general, the more people involved, the more productive the exercise.

Setting
A private room with enough wall space to hang eight sheets of flip chart paper in four separate locations—the more space between these locations, the better

Materials
- Bell or whistle
- Flip chart paper and markers
- Tape (unless you're using self-stick flip chart paper)
- Stopwatch or timer

FACILITATING THE EXERCISE

1. To prepare the exercise, tape two pieces of flip chart paper side by side (see illustration) at four locations around the room; these locations should be as far apart as possible.

2. Across the top of the first two side-by-side sheets, write the headline *Easy*. At the second location, write the headline *Medium*. At the third, *Challenging*. And at the last location, *Leadership*.

   Circle back to the first location. On the left sheet, below the headline, write *Activities*. On the right sheet, write *How to Move Board Members Up to the Next Level* (see illustration). Repeat at the remaining three locations.

EASY	
Activities	*How to Move Board Members Up to the Next Level*

3. Divide your colleagues into groups of three to five and ask each group to start the exercise at one of the four flip chart paper locations.

4. Hand out a few markers to each group with the following instructions:

"When I say go, brainstorm and write fundraising activities on the page where you're standing, paying attention to the level: easy, medium, challenging, or leadership. For example, an easy activity might be addressing envelopes for your fundraising mailing.

"A challenging activity, on the other hand, might be meeting with a donor and asking for a big gift.

"It's worth noting that what one person considers easy another person might consider challenging. Because this is a brainstorm, don't worry too much about this—we can always move the pieces around when we're done.

"Also brainstorm and write notes on the second sheet: How to Move Board Members Up to the Next Level—for example, moving them from the easy level to the medium level. What strategies can we use to encourage a board member to take on more difficult fundraising tasks? You'll find that many of your answers will be general, such as training and mentoring, but you might come up with more specific suggestions as well.

"After three minutes, I'll ring the bell [or blow the whistle]. At that point, all groups rotate clockwise to the next station. You can add to the work of the previous group and amend any ideas, but you can't cross out anything. By the end of the exercise, you'll have had a chance to work at all four locations.

"Questions? Please begin now."

Three minutes per location is an estimate—if groups are being productive, you can give them another minute or two, but *don't* let things drag.

5. Once the exercise is complete, ask everyone to circle the room one more time to review the completed sheets.

6. Gather the full group together to debrief using some combination of the following questions:

   - When you take a look at everything we wrote, what themes or common threads do you see?
   - Let's go around and everyone tell me one thing you learned from this exercise.
   - When you look at these four stations, at what level do you see yourself: easy, medium, challenging, or leadership?
   - Name one activity you would be willing to do.

7. Recruit a volunteer to gather the flip chart paper—or use a smartphone camera—and type the notes for discussion at your next board meeting.

TRAINING TIP If you're working with a group for a long time, schedule this activity when their collective energy is likely to be low—for example, right after lunch (trainers call this "the dead hour") or at the end of the day. Activities that require people to move around can raise the energy level high enough to add thirty to sixty productive minutes to your training.

Creating a Board Fundraising Menu

This exercise reduces resistance by helping people move past the idea that fundraising only means "asking for money." You can create a menu of ways all board members or other volunteers can participate in fundraising, even if they're unwilling to be "askers." For more excitement, structure this activity as a contest—with prizes—and raise the energy level.

This activity provides a nice complement to the Cycle of Fundraising exercise on page 41. The materials created in that activity can be used for this one, too.

Why Do This Exercise?
The worst fundraising strategies are rigid: everyone is expected to do the same things—for example, sell ten raffle tickets or buy five gift memberships. The menu model encourages board members to choose the activities that best meet their needs, interests, and limitations.

Use This Exercise When
You want your board to design their own fundraising opportunities

Time Required
30 to 45 minutes

Audience
The leadership team for your fundraising campaign: some combination of board, staff, and volunteers

Setting
You'll need a room large enough for several small groups—or perhaps several adjacent rooms

Materials
- Stopwatch or timer
- Bell or whistle
- Flip chart paper and markers
- Cycle of fundraising chart (page 44)
- Sample board fundraising menu (page 81)
- Sample board fundraising agreement (page 82)
- Optional: a prize for a member of the winning team

FACILITATING THE EXERCISE

1. Review the Cycle of Fundraising (page 44) with your group, emphasizing how fundraising involves a full sequence of activities and not just soliciting gifts. If you like, pass out copies of the board fundraising menu from the Ohio Environmental Council on page 81 to help clarify the goal of the

exercise. (When the exercise begins, ask them to put it away.) Once the menu is created for your organization, board members will be expected to select activities—one appetizer, one entrée, one dessert—to form their personalized fundraising commitments for the year.

2. Sort the participants into small groups of four to eight. Provide each group with a sheet of flip chart paper and several markers. Have them move to different corners of the room for privacy while they brainstorm.

3. Provide the following instructions: "Your job is to brainstorm all the different ways board members or other volunteers can assist with any sort of fundraising. You can include big-picture tasks, such as creating a fundraising plan, all the way down to micro tasks, like addressing envelopes for the fundraising mailing. Write your ideas on the flip charts.

   "You'll have three minutes to complete this brainstorm—three minutes! This is a contest: the group with the most items in three minutes will be entered into a drawing to win a fabulous prize. Any questions? OK, on your mark ... get set ... go!"

4. When about one minute remains, shout out, "One minute! One minute to go!"

5. As time expires, ring the bell or blow the whistle. Ask the groups to count up the items on their sheets, but don't announce the totals yet.

6. Then provide the following instruction: "Review the list together and mark off the seven or eight items that board members or other volunteers could do that would be most productive and most helpful to the organization." Give them a few minutes to complete this task.

7. Ask each group to select a spokesperson who will report their top tasks. Reconvene the large group to hear these reports. Depending on the number of small groups, you will likely end up with 12 to 20 unduplicated "most helpful" items, which should form the basis for an excellent board fundraising menu.

8. Ask for each group to shout out the total number of items in their brainstorm. Everyone in the winning group gets a slip of paper to write their name. Pick a winner. Provide an appropriate prize: a meal at your favorite restaurant, a book (a fundraising book?), a favorite local food, perhaps a T-shirt or coffee mug from your organization.

9. Debrief using the following questions:

    - What did you learn from this exercise?
    - Did you brainstorm any tasks that surprised you? If so, which ones?
    - What are one or two things from this list that you might be willing to do?

    Be gentle; don't push people to make commitments they're not ready to make. Use words like "might" or "consider" rather than asking them to make firm commitments at this stage.

10. Recruit a volunteer to collect the flip chart sheets—or use a smartphone camera—and create the board fundraising menu you've just developed.

At your next board meeting, follow up by circulating the menu and asking board members to sign up for tasks they're willing to do. The Board/Volunteer Fundraising Agreement form on page 82 is a useful tool for recording their commitments.

> **TRAINING TIP** Keep time, but don't be rigid. We suggest three minutes, but if you sense a lot of energy in the room—if the groups are continuing to generate new ideas—it's fine to let the exercise run longer, since no one else will be keeping time anyway. Just don't let it drag on.

OHIO
ENVIRONMENTAL
COUNCIL
KEEP WATCH, TAKE ACTION, MAKE CHANGE

Board Member: _____   *Date:* _____

Menu of Fundraising Opportunities

This is an "all-you-can-eat" menu!
We ask you to commit to as many items as you like—but at least one per category.

APPETIZERS

1   Provide names of donor prospects
2   Sign & personalize letters to current and prospective donors
3   Attend and mingle with donors at a House Party
4   Promote and attend the Green Gala and mingle with donors

ENTRÉES

5   Significantly increase your annual OEC gift
6   Include the OEC in your estate plan
7   Host a House Party
8   Accompany staff on donor visits
9   Recruit Green Gala sponsors
10   Recruit new board members with fundraising experience and connections
11   Introduce your HR department to Earth Share Ohio or Community Shares of Central Ohio
12   Solicit art, sponsors, or attendees for the Art & Environment Fundraiser

DESSERTS

13   Collect copies of other organizations' published donor lists
14   Make thank you calls to donors
15   Acquire or donate silent auction item donations for the Green Gala
16   Participate in a phone-a-thon to renew members
17   Attend the Art & Environment Fundraiser

Board / Volunteer Fundraising Agreement

Name _____ Date _____

To support the mission of our organization, I agree to take on the following:

1. My gift: $_____   Payment completed by (date) _____

Terms of payment (check, credit card, installments, etc.) _____
_____

2. Prospects. I will provide names and contact information for _____ prospects
by _____ (date). Even if I am unable to follow up with all of these people personally,
I will still add names to the list for mailings, event invitations, etc.

3. My fundraising support tasks (*taken from our fundraising menu*):

a. Activity_____
Date(s) _____ Projected revenue (if applicable) $_____
Help/support needed from staff or board _____
_____

b. Activity_____
Date(s) _____ Projected revenue (if applicable) $_____
Help/support needed from staff or board _____
_____

c. Activity_____
Date(s) _____ Projected revenue (if applicable) $_____
Help/support needed from staff or board _____
_____

_____   _____
Signature of board member or volunteer   Signature of board chair

Board Giving: What's The Right Amount?

Some nonprofits set quotas for board giving. For example, each trustee is asked to give a personal gift of $1,000. Other boards have a "give or get" policy. They set a minimum goal for individual board members, who are expected to bring in that amount through a combination of personal giving and solicitations.

We're uncomfortable with these models for two reasons:

a) The best boards include all socioeconomic levels: poor, middle-income, and wealthy people working together, representing the diversity of the community. Setting a minimum level for personal giving—especially if it's a big number—can price some people out of board service.

b) Under the "give or get" scenario, board members with resources can write a check and sit on the sidelines while others put in the effort to raise money from others.

These scenarios are inherently inequitable. Therefore, we believe in a "give AND get" policy. This exercise focuses on the "give" portion of the equation.

Consider the following language from a board agreement: "Because you're a leader in this organization, we expect to be one of your *top three charitable commitments* while you're on the board." This provision allows everyone to make a gift that is significant to them. Furthermore, as this exercise demonstrates, we suggest a collective goal for board giving, rather than focusing on individual commitments.

Why Do This Exercise?
Because there's karma in fundraising—if you want your trustees to be effective fundraisers, they must give first

Use This Exercise When
You are creating your annual budget and want to set a goal for board giving

Time Required
15 minutes

Audience
Your board

Setting
Anywhere your board meets, preferably around a table

Materials
Paper and pens

FACILITATING THE EXERCISE

1. Ask your board, "If we pooled our gifts for one year and calculated the total, how much should that be? What's our target?"

    A thoughtful board member will ask for a baseline amount: "How much did we give last year?" Have that number available. Then pose the question, "Are we comfortable with that amount? Do we want to aim higher? Is there any reason to set a lower goal?"

2. Once you've agreed on a collective number, it's easy to test. Hand out pieces of paper and ask each person to write their high and low gift levels: the smallest and largest amount they expect to give to your organization this year. DO NOT ask them to write their names. Then ask participants to fold the papers in half to guarantee anonymity.

3. Collect the papers, step out of the room, add up the numbers, then come back in and announce the collective high and low targets for total board giving.

4. If the total number for board giving falls short of your goal, you may find yourself facilitating another round of conversation. This is healthy, since you're now debating a real number based on real data. Give your board members the time they need to either set a new goal or confirm the one they've already chosen. Encourage them to be realistic in their giving, rather than choose an amount they won't be able to fulfill.

5. To debrief the exercise, ask the following questions:

    *   Do we want to establish a specific board giving goal for this year?
    *   As a board, do we want to aim for the high end or the low end?
    *   Do we want to adopt a participation goal as well? In other words, should we expect every board member to contribute financially?

If you're planning a capital campaign, you can also use this exercise to identify or confirm a collective board giving goal for the campaign.

Last, we encourage you to include a line item in your budget titled "Board Giving." Every budget review becomes an opportunity to track progress toward the annual goal. Fundraising staff members love this line item. If there's a discrepancy between the columns marked "Projected Income" and "Income to Date," the board has to take responsibility and can't simply assign staff to solve the problem.

TRAINING TIP Because this may be a controversial topic—easily shot down by a few vocal board members—be strategic about how and when you propose a collective, firm goal for board giving.

First, check in with a few supportive trustees in advance and ask them to speak in favor when the idea of a board giving goal is raised at the next board meeting. Second, recruit a generous board member to raise the topic—ideally someone who isn't perceived to be wealthy but chooses to give a significant donation based on his or her capacity. Perhaps you can secure a challenge gift (again, in advance) based on total board giving. Do what you can to create incentives and anticipate objections so you're positioned to make the strongest possible case.

What You Measure Is What You Get

 00:30

Many fundraising programs track only the amount of money raised. While it's natural to focus on money, tracking and measuring other outcomes often leads to raising more money. This exercise will help you and your board members expand your ideas about what to track. As your conception of measurement expands, you may notice a greater focus on building strong relationships with your donors.

Why Do This Exercise?
To demonstrate many of the ways that fundraising is not about money

Use This Exercise When
Developing your fundraising plan or setting goals

Time Required
About 20 minutes

Audience
Insiders: the people who help to plan and oversee your fundraising program

Setting
Anywhere you gather to work on your campaign plan and train your participants

Materials
Flip chart paper and markers

FACILITATING THE EXERCISE

1. Set the stage by telling your board or committee members that before you create fundraising goals based on last year's performance, you'd like to explore the idea of non-monetary goals.

2. Ask whether anyone in the group has worked with organizations that measure and track the progress of outcomes that aren't financial. Examples might include customer satisfaction, number of homes built, employee retention, and people who remain clean and sober after treatment.

3. Ask the group to generate a list of all of the non-monetary items you might track for your fund development plan. Write them on the flip chart. The list could include the number of:

   - Volunteers assisting with fundraising
   - In-person asks

- Upgrades: donors who increase their gifts over last year
- Donors who make personal visits to your work site to learn more about your work
- Turnaround time on thank you letters

If you're patient, your group will come up with a robust list.

4. To debrief this exercise, ask the following questions:

- If we set goals for some of the non-financial aspects of the fundraising program—for example, _____ [choose one or two items from the list]—what impact would it have?
- Ask each person to choose three or four items they'd like to measure in the fundraising plan and to describe why they chose them.

TRAINING TIP As facilitator, your job is to make sure everyone gets their fair share of "air time." If you have individuals who tend to take over, find polite but firm ways to invite the voices of the quieter participants. One strategy: "Let's go around the circle and have everyone speak to this question for no more than thirty seconds. If you have nothing to add, just say 'I pass.'" Another strategy: "On this round, let's limit the comments to anyone who hasn't spoken yet."

Building a Gift Chart

As the saying goes, if you don't have a goal, you won't get there. This exercise will help you identify how many gifts at different amounts are required to reach your goal. It's also a quick and easy way to familiarize your board members, volunteers, and coworkers with the basic principles of fundraising math. When someone says, "We've set a goal of $50,000; now let's find 50 people to give $1,000 each," you can say, "Your math is impeccable, but that's not how fundraising works. Let me show you why."

Why Do This Exercise?
Everyone on your fundraising team needs to understand the basics, and some of that knowledge is imparted through this exercise

Use This Exercise When
You're ready to set a goal for your fundraising campaign

Time Required
30 minutes

Audience
Two to four leaders of your fundraising campaign: some combination of board, staff, and volunteers

Setting
A private room with a table large enough to accommodate up to five people

Materials
- Flip chart paper and markers
- Calculator
- Sample gift charts from Toxics Action Center and Five Valleys Land Trust (pages 90 and 91)

FACILITATING THE EXERCISE

Before beginning this exercise, photocopy the sample gift charts on pages 90 and 91.

1. In most donor fundraising campaigns, the mix of contributions looks something like this:

    10 percent of the donors yield 60 percent of the money
    20 percent of the donors yield 20 percent of the money
    70 percent of the donors yield 20 percent of the money

    In other words, most organizations rely on a handful of major donors to generate the bulk of their unrestricted income. Create a simplified version of this graphic on a flip chart as follows:

Donors		**Dollars**
10%	=	60%
20%	=	20%
70%	=	20%

Explain that the purpose of this exercise is to create a gift chart (sometimes called a gift table or gift pyramid) by setting a goal and then calculating how many donations at each level you'll need to reach that goal.

2. Pass around the samples. Give people a few moments to review them.

3. To build the chart, start by setting a campaign goal. Assume that your largest donation (or "lead gift") needs to equal 10 percent to 20 percent of the goal, and your second-tier gifts will be 5 percent to 10 percent of the goal. Using the math outlined above and the samples, construct your gift pyramid on flip chart paper. Recruit one person to help with the calculator while everyone discusses and decides on the appropriate gift levels.

    While this isn't designed as a prospecting exercise (see chapter 5), it might be useful to emphasize that for each gift, you'll need between two and four prospects, because many choose not to contribute at all or contribute at lower levels. Therefore, you must identify many more prospects than the number of gifts needed to fill in the chart and finish the campaign.

4. Debrief the exercise by asking the following questions:

    *   How do we feel about the goal? Should it be lower or higher?
    *   Have we chosen a lead gift that is large enough to force us to stretch?
    *   We will have a prospecting session later, but at first glance, do we know people we can approach for contributions at the top three levels?

Once you create the chart, you can test its feasibility with the Rating Your Prospects exercise on page 120.

> **TRAINING TIP** Note that this exercise requires a small team rather than a large group. Given the common discomfort with all things mathematical, choose participants who have some facility with math (percentages and ratios) or are unafraid to jump in and improve their skills. Those with fundraising experience will also be useful.

TOXICS ACTION CENTER

Goal: $100,000

Gifts Needed	Gifts In Hand	Gift Amount	Category Total	TOTAL
1	☒ *F. Smith*	$10,000	$10,000	$10,000
3	☒☒☐ *C. Goldstein; D. Lee*	$5,000	$15,000	$25,000
7	☐☐☐☐☐☐☐	$2,500	$17,500	$42,500
12	☒☒☒☒☐ ☐☐☐☐☐☐ *M. Cook; R. Rodriguez; A. Bielecki; R. Robinson; B. Fields*	$1,500	$18,000	$60,500
22	☒☒☒☒☐☐☐☐☐☐ ☐☐☐☐☐☐☐☐☐☐☐☐ *M. Fischer; R. Waterman; L. Jones; S. Nguyen*	$1,000	$22,000	$82,500
35	☒☒☒☒☒☒☒☒☒☒☒ ☒☒☒☒☒☒☒☒☐☐☐ ☐☐☐☐☐☐☐☐☐☐☐ *P. Patel; J. Hermann; M. Smith; A. Farnham; F. Murphy; K. Saenz; P. Newman; F. Gold; J. Davenport; S. Jayapal; R. Muhammed; D. Cohen; J. Miller; F. Yamamoto; C. Hickock; R. Schmook; l. Bean; K. Lieu; K. Delmarva; R. Washington; D. Best*	$500	$17,500	**$100,000**

Adapted from Toxics Action Center; names have been changed. Used with permission.

FIVE
VALLEYS
LAND
TRUST

STEWARDSHIP CHALLENGE 2009
Goal: $250,000

Committed to date (8/25/09): $130,351
■ = committed gift

Gifts Needed	Gifts or Pledges in Hand	Gift Amount	Category Total	CUMMULATIVE TOTAL
5	■■□□□	$10,001 - $25,000	$75,000	$75,000
8	■□□□□ □□□	$5,001 - $10,000	$50,000	$125,000
20	■■■■■ ■■□□□ □□□□□ □□□□□	$2,501 - $5,000	$60,000	$185,000
20	■■■■■ ■□□□□ □□□□□ □□□□□	$1,001 - $2,500	$30,000	$215,000
30	■■■■■■ ■■■■■■ ■■■■■■ ■■□□□□ □□□□□□	$500 - $1,000	$20,000	$235,000
	346 gifts	$499 or less	$15,000	$250,000

Creating a Twelve-Week Major Gifts Campaign

This activity takes a good idea—"Let's do a major gifts campaign!"—and translates it into specific tasks and deadlines. By doing this exercise, your participants will better understand the scope of the campaign and how the pieces fit together. It's also a great opportunity for problem solving and team building.

There's nothing magical about twelve weeks; some organizations can complete these tasks in six, eight, or ten weeks. (We know of one organization that shuts down the office and completes most of this work in two weeks.) Regardless, this is an exercise for creating a time-limited, focused campaign rather than a major donor program that continues throughout the year. Both models have strengths and weaknesses, and each organization needs to decide on the best approach given its needs, opportunities, and organizational culture.

Why Do This Exercise?
Without a calendar, a plan is not a plan

Use This Exercise When
You are planning your major gift campaign

Time Required
30 minutes for the exercise, plus 60 minutes in advance to prepare the materials

Audience
The leadership team for your fundraising campaign: some combination of board, staff, and volunteers. This exercise can be done with as few as three participants and as many as a dozen.

Setting
A room with 10 to 15 feet of blank wall space and enough room for participants to move around in front of the wall. You'll be putting Post-It notes on the wall, so you need a surface that will hold these sticky notes.

Materials
- Two packs of large (8 inches by 6 inches) Post-It notes
- Markers (non-toxic)
- You may want a camera to record the finished calendar

PREPARATION

1. Using markers, write Week 1, Week 2, all the way to Week 12 on twelve Post-It notes or "cards." These serve as your calendar for the exercise. Write large enough that people can read the cards from several feet away.

2. Prepare Post-Its listing the following tasks in a major gifts campaign. Note that some tasks can take place several times during the campaign and therefore require several cards.

- Identify campaign leadership
- Set campaign dollar goal
- Prepare gift chart
- Identify challenge gift
- Identify prospectors to suggest names
- Identify prospects
- "Rate prospects" for dollar amount
- Test and modify goal: enough prospects?
- Identify askers
- Test and modify goal: enough askers?
- Assign prospects
- Train askers
- Create campaign calendar
- Prepare campaign materials
- Create lines of accountability
- Prepare letters to prospects
- Send letters (make three of these Post-Its)
- Phone prospects to schedule (three of these)
- Meet with prospects (three of these)
- Follow-up calls to undecided prospects (two of these)
- Check-in meeting with leadership and askers (two of these)
- Thank donors (two of these)
- Wrap-up meeting to evaluate campaign
- Identify leadership for next campaign
- Celebration
- Four blank Post-It notes

FACILITATING THE EXERCISE

1. Place calendar cards (Week 1 through Week 12) in a horizontal line across the wall. Put them high, as the team will be placing tasks cards below.

2. Off to the side, place the task cards on the wall in random order. Be sure to shuffle them well.

3. Invite everyone to step up and begin placing the cards on what they consider appropriate spots on the calendar. Encourage them to ignore a card if they decide the task isn't needed, or add other steps by writing on the blank Post-It notes.

4. Once the cards are placed, ask everyone to stand back and look at the entire calendar and continue to move the pieces as needed.

5. Reconvene the group and debrief the exercise using the following questions:

   - This campaign includes a lot of specific steps. Does this level of detail make you feel empowered or overwhelmed? Why? Give people a chance to discuss, making note of how many fall into each camp. If a large majority feels overwhelmed, you may have to simplify the campaign and reduce the number of steps.
   - Do you believe this campaign model would work for us? Why or why not? How do we adapt it to make it work?
   - What's our next step?

   Note: In most fundraising campaigns, the two most significant limiting factors are the number of prospects and the number of askers who will engage these prospects. The cards marked "Test and modify goal: enough prospects?" and "Test and modify goal: enough askers?" are sometimes misunderstood, but the intention is simple enough: to ensure that you have critical mass in both of these areas before proceeding. Here's a hint: place these two cards fairly early on your calendar so you will know, early on, if your goal is realistic.

6. Once you've reached consensus on the calendar, record your work. A camera is the handiest way to do this. Should you choose to go forward with a campaign, the photo will serve as your campaign calendar.

There is no single correct solution to completing this exercise. If you need guidance, see page 95 for a sample campaign calendar.

There is no single correct solution to completing this exercise. If you need guidance, see page 95 for a sample campaign calendar.

TRAINING TIP As everyone works together (or not) to build the calendar, pay attention to the process. Some will jump in and start moving cards around; others will stand back and watch. Some will ask for help or suggestions; others will work alone. How people work during this exercise can teach you a lot about the way your group will work together once the actual campaign begins. One of the functions of a facilitator is to help bring meaning to these exercises. During the debriefing, describe what you've seen—name it gently and respectfully, but name it.

Sample 12-Week Major Gifts Campaign Calendar

Week 1	Week 2	Week 3	Week 4	Week 5	Week 6	Week 7	Week 8	Week 9	Week 10	Week 11	Week 12
ID campaign leadership	Prepare gift chart	ID prospects	Train askers	Send letters	Meet with prospects	Send letters	Meet with prospects	Send letters	Meet with prospects	Follow-up calls to undecided prospects	Wrap-up meeting to evaluate campaign
Set $ goal	ID prospectors to suggest names	"Rate prospects" for $ amount	Assign prospects	Phone prospects to schedule	Thank donors	Phone prospects to schedule	Follow-up calls to undecided prospects	Phone prospects to schedule	Check-in meeting with leaders and askers		ID leadership for next campaign
ID challenge gift	ID askers	Test and modify goal: enough prospects?	Create lines of accountability			Check-in meeting with leaders and askers	Thank donors		Thank donors		Celebration!
Create campaign calendar	Prepare campaign materials	Test and modify goal: enough askers?	Prepare letters to prospects								

How Many Relationships Can You Manage?

Far too often, we treat our donors like ATMs: every contact is about extracting money. If you're planning a fundraising campaign—especially a major donor effort—it's important to think strategically about keeping donors informed and involved. By focusing on assignments and time commitments, this activity helps create structure and accountability.

This exercise works best if it follows the Cycle of Fundraising, which you'll find on page 41.

Why Do This Exercise?
To create a specific task-and-time list for strengthening outreach to donors

Use This Exercise When
You want to reality-test the number of donor relationships you can actively manage

Time Required
30-45 minutes

Audience
Anyone involved with your fundraising campaign: some combination of board, staff, and volunteers—especially those who are preparing to meet with donors

Setting
Anywhere you gather to work on your campaign plan and train your participants

Materials
- Flip chart paper and markers
- Completed worksheet: Cycle of Fundraising: Building a Donor Engagement Menu (page 46)

FACILITATING THE EXERCISE

1. Review the completed Cycle of Fundraising worksheet (page 46), focusing on the box labeled, "Involve Donors More Deeply." Talk through the items included in this box, such as "Invite to lunch," "Email updates," and "Volunteer opportunities." Ask if participants have questions about any of these items. If it seems fruitful, encourage the group to add to the list.

2. Discuss with the group how much time each task will take and then assign an amount of time per task, per donor, per year. Depending on the number of people present, you can discuss this with the full group or break into smaller groups.

For example, your list might include the task "Meet donor for coffee." Assuming two meetings per year for the average major donor and two hours to schedule, travel, conduct each donor meeting and make notes afterward, the time allocated for this task would be four hours per year per donor. See the sample task list below.

Task	Number of contacts per year	Time per contact, including scheduling and travel	Total time per year
Meet donor for coffee	2	2 hours	4 hours
Email updates	12	10 minutes	2 hours
Tour our facility	1	1.5 hours	1.5 hours
Add your own tasks			

3. Once you've determined the amount of time for each task, write the time on the flip chart. Add up the numbers. You have a rough estimate of the number of hours per year needed to involve and engage an average donor.

    Since every donor is different and requires varying levels of engagement, the total hours will be only a rough estimate—but a rough estimate beats a wild guess. The process of thinking through this question will help your volunteers figure out how many donors they can realistically engage during the year.

4. Write the names of your fundraising team members on another flip chart page. Ask them, "How many hours per month do you have available to spend on donor relationships?"—then multiply by twelve. Write the annual number of hours after each name.

Team member	Hours available per month	Hours available per year	Number of relationships to manage
Sally			
Consuela			
Rocky			
Thomas			

5. From here, it's an easy step to answer the question "How many relationships can you manage?" Divide the number after each team member by the total number of hours per year it takes to engage a donor. For example, if your average donor requires 12 hours annually, and Sally has 36 hours per year available, Sally should be assigned no more than three relationships.

6. To debrief this exercise, ask the following questions:
   - Looking at the chart, does the number of relationships assigned to you seem realistic?
   - With the understanding that each donor is different, how do we customize this list? For example, we know Mildred doesn't use email—what do we do with her instead?
   - What systems do we need to have in place to hold each other accountable?

The best time to conduct this exercise is before you finalize your campaign goal and gift chart. Too many organizations solicit donations without having a plan to keep their donors involved or knowing how much time it'll take. When these relationships are neglected, supporters start to feel ignored, which is a self-defeating way to run a fundraising program. This exercise gives you the tools to design a better strategy.

TRAINING TIP As you facilitate this exercise, the trick is to keep people focused on the details without arguing about them. For example, does a donor lunch take an hour or ninety minutes ... and does it really matter if you get this question right or wrong?

If you spend too much time at the wrong level of detail, your session will descend into chaos. Remember, your goal is to come up with a credible estimate of the time needed each year to involve a donor—with an emphasis on the word estimate.

It might help to frame this activity as an experiment. As noted above, even if you can't develop or agree on specific numbers, the process of working through this question—how many hours do we need to set aside for each important relationship?—reinforces in a very specific way that fundraising isn't just asking for money, and that most of the work happens after you receive the gift.

Fundraising on Steroids: A Fundraising Game

This game uses money people have in their wallets and purses—no extra funds required! Participants will experience and reflect on what makes a fundraising campaign successful—and then everyone gets their money back. It's light-hearted but has the potential to deliver several important fundraising lessons.

Why Do This Exercise?
It's a simple, interactive way to create shared knowledge about fundraising campaigns and what makes them work

Use This Exercise When
You are ready to launch a campaign and you want your volunteers thinking about what motivates people to give

Time Required
45 minutes

Audience
Some combination of board,

fundraising committee, and staff— ideally at least 15 people.

Setting
A room large enough to accommodate small groups of five to eight, each sitting around a separate table

Materials
- Stopwatch or timer
- Bell or whistle
- Flip chart paper and markers
- Paper and pens
- Discussion questions (see below and page 102) for the facilitator at each table

FACILITATING THE EXERCISE

1. Before beginning this exercise, prepare sheets with the discussion questions (see item 5 below) or post them on the flip chart. Cover the questions so you can reveal them when needed.

2. Divide everyone into groups of five to eight and ask for three volunteers at each table to play specific roles:

   - The *campaign chair* will organize a ten-minute campaign to raise at least $100.

- The *banker* will write donor names and gift amounts in the order received.
- The *facilitator* will debrief the exercise and report to the full group at the end.

3. Instruct everyone to take out their wallets and prepare to make a campaign gift using cash, credit cards, or hand-written pledges. Let everyone know this is a game and they WILL get their money back.

4. Tell the campaign chairs they have exactly ten minutes to raise at least $100 for the annual fund. Ring the bell to start the campaign. Keep close track of time. When two minutes remain, give a warning. At ten minutes, ring the bell to stop the exercise.

5. Hand the discussion questions (page 102) to the facilitators at each table, letting them know their group has ten minutes.

   a) **Amount raised.** Did you reach your goal? Why or why not?
   b) **Gift amounts and sequence.** Review the gift amounts and the order received. Did the sequence make a difference?
   c) **Leadership.** What was the role of the campaign chair? How did her or his actions influence the total you raised?
   d) **Lessons learned.** What lessons did you learn from this exercise?

6. Reconvene the large group. Ask each facilitator to report the lessons learned at his or her table, writing them on the flip chart as they report. Common lessons include:

   - Specific fundraising goals and timetables are helpful
   - People decide on their gifts, in part, by seeing what others give
   - It's inspiring when the campaign chair gives first
   - Challenge gifts are effective

   Capture the core ideas on a flip chart while each table reports.

7. Debrief the exercise by asking how you might apply these lessons to your fundraising program.

A note about this exercise: You may wonder if someone will simply throw down $100, leaving the group to sit in silence. In practice, if someone puts in the entire amount, others will suggest raising the goal and will add their own gifts because they don't want to be left out. The generosity of others inspires people to give more.

TRAINING TIP When facilitating a complex exercise, provide instructions in a step-by step fashion; this one has three parts. First, let people know they'll be playing a game using real money that will be returned after the game is over. Then divide them in the simplest way into small groups. Finally, once they're arranged at their tables, give specific instructions for how to begin the game. By guiding them one step at a time, you bring the participants along and minimize confusion that can lead to resistance.

Fundraising on Steroids

DISCUSSION QUESTIONS

A. **Amount raised.** Did you reach your goal? Why or why not?

B. **Gift amounts and sequence.** Review gift amounts and the order in which they came in. Did the sequence make a difference in how much money was raised?

C. **Leadership.** What was the role of the campaign chair? How did her or his actions influence the total you raised?

D. **Lessons learned.** What are three key lessons you learned from this process?

PART 5

FINDING PEOPLE TO ASK

One of the most common misconceptions about fundraising is that philanthropy comes from "famous rich people I don't know." According to Giving USA, the annual bible of fundraising research, roughly 70 percent of American households contribute to nonprofits. Seven out of ten people you know—your friends, neighbors, colleagues—give to charitable causes. Volunteer hours aren't included in this calculation; we're talking cold, hard cash.

People with modest incomes can and do make substantial gifts. Recent data show that total giving per household averages between $1,300 and $2,000 per year. Among the two-thirds of Americans who take the standard deduction on their income taxes—primarily middle-class, working-class, and poor people—average annual donations total more than $500 per family.

We hear a lot about Buffett and Turner and Gates, but a lot less about Smith, Sanchez, Lee, Nguyen, and Jones. They may not give multimillion dollar gifts, but, taken as a group, they are the most predictable and reliable donors.

If you're looking for good prospects—generous people who care about your issues—they're right in your neighborhood. They're sitting next to you on the bus, the train, the plane ... and they're stuck in traffic, too. If you have a job, you work with them. If you enjoy sports, you play with them (or maybe you sit on the couch and drink beer with them). If you participate in a religious community, you pray with them. You interact with donors every day—and many of them give more money than you imagine.

You know the old line about the streets being paved with gold? Surprise—this is one myth that's actually true, because philanthropists are *everywhere*. This chapter provides you with the tools and training to find them.

Fundraising from the Inside Out

Prospecting is one of the basic techniques used to identify potential donors. This simple exercise offers a strategy—one of several included in this book—to teach your board and staff to think like fundraisers.

Why Do This Exercise?
The work of our nonprofits touches so many people, and many would give if asked

Use This Exercise When
You want to help your board and staff identify and prioritize existing donors and new prospects

Time Required
10-15 minutes

Audience
Anyone involved with your fundraising campaign: some combination of board, staff, and volunteers

Setting
A space large enough to accommodate several small groups of three to five each

Materials
Flip chart paper and markers

FACILITATING THE EXERCISE

1. Draw three or four concentric circles on the flip chart paper—it looks like a target—so that the largest circle touches the edge of the paper.

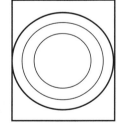

2. Say to your colleagues, "This diagram represents the universe of our organization. Those who are closest to our mission and work, such as our board and the staff, are at the center." Write the words *Board* and *Staff* inside the center circle. "Out here on the fringe is the broader community." Write the words *Broader Community* or *General Public* outside the outer circle.

"Our job is to brainstorm the groups of people that might be interested in our work; for example, one group might be the people we serve. As you mention the groups, I'll write them on the chart. Those who are most connected go closer to the center; those who are less connected will be placed further out."

3. As the brainstorming begins, do your best to write all the groups, placing them in the appropriate circle. You can always ask the group for help: "How close to the center would you place local businesses?" Keep encouraging more responses until you fill up the paper.

4. Once the brainstorming is complete, pick up two other markers of different colors. With one, draw several arrows that begin in the center and radiate outward in different directions. "The *strategy* of fundraising," you say, "is always inside out. We start with our best prospects first—those who are most committed and connected to the organization."

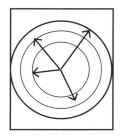

5. Take the second colored marker and draw several arrows that begin around the outside and end up in the central circle. "The goal of fundraising," you say, "is outside in. Our goal is to pull everyone toward the center of the circle—to deepen their connection and commitment to our work."

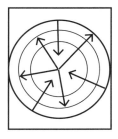

6. To debrief this exercise, ask the following questions:

   • Looking at the chart, which constituencies do we do a good job of engaging? Which ones would benefit from more attention?
   • What strategies might we use to move people closer to the center?
   • What experiences have you had with nonprofits that moved you closer to the center and strengthened your connection to the group?

TRAINING TIP If you have time, this is a great moment to introduce the ABCs of Identifying Prospects exercise, which follows on page 106, and have your colleagues begin to generate names for your fundraising campaign. Consider reserving enough time to do both activities back to back.

The ABCs of Identifying Prospects

Everyone knows potential donors—even people who say, "I don't know any-one who has money." Indeed, the average adult has relationships of some sort with 150 to 200 people (we're not even including social media "friends"), and about 70 percent of those people support charitable organizations. This exer-cise provides a systematic way of sorting through your relationships to iden-tify prospects.

Why Do This Exercise?
To help address the myth that "philanthropy comes from wealthy strangers that I don't know"

Use This Exercise When
You want your board, staff, and volunteers to help expand your prospect pool or deepen outreach to current donors

Time Required
20 minutes

Audience
Anyone involved with your

fundraising campaign: some combination of board, staff, and volunteers

Setting
Anywhere you gather to work on your campaign plan and train your participants—preferably with people sitting in a circle or around a table

Materials
- Flip chart paper and markers
- Prospect Form (page 109)

FACILITATING THE EXERCISE

1. Introduce this exercise by telling participants you want their help with thinking about current donors and also expanding the pool of potential donors. Let them know that, while you'll be asking for names of people they know, no one will solicit these prospects without the permission or involvement of the recommender.

2. Write the following on the flip chart:
   ACCESS
   BELIEF
   CAPACITY

3. Explain that these are the three criteria for identifying prospects.

ACCESS: Do they have a relationship with any of our board members, staff, donors, or key volunteers? Are they already contributing money, time, or both to our organization?

BELIEF: Do they care about our issues or programs, or those who benefit from our work? Some organizations have broad appeal, while others will appeal to a narrower group of people.

CAPACITY: Are they charitable? Do they give to other organizations?

People who meet these three criteria are legitimate *prospects* and should be asked to contribute (or perhaps asked to contribute more). Note that the ABC formula makes it easier to remember the definition of the word *prospect*.

4. Emphasize that the order listed above—access, belief, capacity—is also the proper ranking when weighing these criteria. To state this differently, the relationship is the most important factor. People who are new to fundraising tend to begin by asking, "Who's rich?" rather than "Who do we know?" This is exactly backwards.

5. Hand out copies of the prospect form (page 109). Talk people through the headings, explaining that:

   a) *Contact.* They should write names, but don't need to include contact information at this time. That will be collected later.

   b) *Relationship to you* is straightforward: friend, coworker, cousin, and the like.

   c) *Believes in cause?* This can be answered with a yes, no, or a question mark. Because you're listing individuals you know, you should have some sense of their values and interests.

   d) *Gives to nonprofits?* This doesn't refer specifically to your organization but rather, "Is this person charitable? Does he or she contribute to nonprofits?" Again, this question can be answered with a yes, no, or a question mark.

   e) *Gives to us?* Has this person ever given to our organization? Use a yes, no, or question mark.

   f) On *Gift range*, encourage participants to either make an educated guess about the amount the prospect might give or leave this column blank if they're completely stumped.

It will be helpful to remind everyone that about 70 percent of Americans contribute to nonprofit organizations, so we can assume that seven out of ten people we know are donors. While this exercise is designed to identify new prospects, let participants know they can also include current donors to be "upgraded" or asked to give a larger donation.

6. Ask them to the leave the first line blank; it will be filled in at the end of the exercise. Then instruct them to sit quietly, flip through their "mental Rolodexes," and begin writing names. Encourage participants who have smartphones, tablets, or other devices to use them, since these devices are full of personal contacts. Allow them about ten minutes to get as far as they can with the prospect form. Some will fill up the form and start writing more names in the margins; others will struggle. It's important to encourage everyone and not make this activity competitive.

7. After ten minutes, ask for attention. On the principle that you can't ask others until you have given yourself—this is one of the basic tenets of fundraising—instruct each person to write his or her own name on the first line and, if they're ready, to include the amount of their gift. Those who are uncomfortable writing the amount of their gifts while others are present can add the amount later.

8. Finally, thank everyone for sharing their names. Suggest a process for adding contact information, collecting the forms, and entering them into your database or creating a master list. For example, ask everyone to bring their completed forms to the next board meeting, where the development committee will collect and compile them.

9. Explain that the next step (for a future meeting) is to talk through the names together and decide how to "segment" them: which prospects will be approached in person, or invited to a house party, or added to the mailing list for appeal letters, or added to the phone bank call list, and so on.

10. Debrief the exercise using the following questions:

   • What was your experience thinking about potential donors? How did you choose to filter people in or out?
   • Has your perspective changed on the question "Who is a prospect?" If so, how?
   • Did this exercise change your thinking about your own giving? If so, how?

We thank our colleagues Kim Klein and Mike Roque for sharing this exercise.

TRAINING TIP You'll get a lot further with this exercise if you've already worked with your team to reduce their resistance to fundraising. Start with Why People Give on page 29.

Prospect Form

Name/contact info	Relationship to me	Believes in cause?	Gives to nonprofits?	Gives to us?	Gift range

Donors All Around Us

If you're involved with a large institution such as a college or hospital, you probably have staff members devoted to donor research. Their work is to identify where donor interests overlap with the institution's mission and determine the giving capacity of donors and prospects. Most nonprofits, however, don't have staff or money for focused donor research—and that's okay.

One of the simplest, least expensive donor-research strategies involves collecting and comparing lists. This exercise uses two kinds of lists: your current donors plus supporters of peer nonprofits. If you compare these lists diligently, we believe you'll find that donors who give $50 to your organization sometimes give $500 or $5,000 to other nonprofits. As you develop a strategy for cultivating and upgrading donors, you can prioritize these individuals for deeper engagement.

Why Do This Exercise?
To broaden your thinking about who might qualify to give a significant gift

Use This Exercise When
You are ready to introduce your board and staff members to a basic, easy-to-use prospect research tool

Time Required
30 minutes

Audience
Anyone involved with your fundraising campaign: some combination of board, staff, and volunteers

Setting
A space large enough to accommodate several small groups of three to five each. Because you'll be discussing donor names and giving amounts, privacy is important.

Materials
- Bell or whistle
- Flip chart paper and markers
- A printed alphabetical list of your top 200 to 400 donors, with donor history information as you're able to produce it—for example, total annual giving, largest gift, and/or what stimulated the gift (a letter, an email request, attendance at an event, a face-to-face ask)
- Published donor lists from peer nonprofits operating in your area. You can find these in nonprofit newsletters, annual reports, event programs, websites, and the like. These lists are often segmented by gift size, which will give you some sense of a prospect's giving potential. (It's worth noting that top-tier gifts most often go to organizations that deeply engage their donors and prospects.)
- Optional: a prize for a member of the winning team

FACILITATING THE EXERCISE

1. Before beginning the exercise, make enough photocopies of all lists so that everyone can have a copy.

2. Have your participants form small groups of three to five. If you have both board and staff present, ask for mixed groups.

3. Explain that this exercise is a contest. The purpose is to identify as many donors as possible who support multiple nonprofits, including your organization. Given the nature of the exercise, everyone must swear the confidentiality oath.

4. Distribute copies of your organization's donor list noting (if you have this information) how people were solicited in the past. If necessary, delete the data for any donors present—perhaps some of your board members?—who may want the amount of their gifts to remain private.

5. Explain that one of the basic principles of fundraising is that donors will give five to ten times more money *in person* than they'll send through the mail, and at least two to three times more money *in person* than they'll give over the phone. These ratios have been tested by many fundraising professionals—including the authors—and confirmed by academic research.

   For example, if you send fundraising appeals through the mail, look at the numbers. Based on our experience and that of many of our peers, someone who gives $100 by mail is likely a $500 to $1,000 prospect, but only if that person agrees to meet. This formula provides a convenient shorthand for upgrading current donors and members.

6. Next, distribute the lists you've collected from peer nonprofits. For example, if you're a conservation organization, gather the lists of other environmental groups in your community or region. If you serve children, look for other local or regional charities that benefit children.

   Note that many of these lists are sorted by gift amount: supporter, benefactor, angel, archangel, and the like. Explain to your colleagues that by reviewing these lists, you can gather useful information about current donors, including if they give (and how much) to other charitable organizations.

7. Explain that they will have about fifteen minutes to review the lists and identify names that appear more than once. The team that comes up with the most recurring names will be entered into a drawing, and one team member will win a prize.

8. Pay attention to the time and the energy in the room. If the groups seem to be winding down, you may want to end this exercises before 15 minutes. When about one minute remains, alert them to wrap up.

9. As time expires, ring the bell or blow the whistle. Ask the groups to count up the number of names that appear more than once and announce the total. Everyone in the winning group receives a slip of paper to write their own name; then pick a winner. Provide an appropriate prize: a meal at your favorite restaurant, a book (a fundraising book?), a favorite local food, perhaps a T-shirt or coffee mug from your organization.

10. To debrief this activity, use the following questions, noting the responses on the flip chart:

    • Did you identify people who give to us already but might be able to give more?
    • Which other names—people who support other organizations but don't yet give to us —did you see most often? Anyone in particular we should prioritize? Why?
    • Is there anybody on these lists that you would be willing to reach out to and try to involve more directly in our work?

    If anyone says yes to this last question, include the names of these potential donors in the Rating Your Prospects exercise on page 120, which you can use to set ask amounts and assign askers.

11. Collect all the lists—reinforcing the confidentiality rule—and recruit someone to help compile the names that appear more than once, along with any giving information included, such as size of gifts to peer nonprofits.

TRAINING TIP When reviewing lists from other nonprofits, people some-times raise concerns about "stealing" or "poaching" donors. If this issue comes up, we suggest two responses. First, once these lists are published, they become public information. Most organizations calculate that the ben-efits of publicly acknowledging their supporters far outweigh the risks.

Second, many contributors give to multiple organizations. As noted in an earlier exercise, Where's the Money? on page 36, a typical donor house-hold supports five to ten organizations per year. So the idea that we can "steal" a donor starts with the assumption of scarcity, which we've been challenging throughout this book. People have free will to give (or not) to as many organizations as they choose, and most givers support multiple groups, causes, and projects.

What's a Major Gift?

For novices, the term "major gifts fundraising" conjures images of wealthy strangers, fancy clothes, expensive liquor, and secret handshakes. This exercise reframes the concept to make it more accessible (and less scary) for smaller organizations. It nicely augments another exercise, the ABCs of Identifying Prospects, that you'll find on page 106.

Why Do This Exercise?
Major donors are everywhere, but they are invisible to most of us—so let's learn to see the world a little differently

Use This Exercise When
You're planning a major gifts campaign and you want your team to think more broadly about who might make a significant gift

Time Required
30 minutes

Audience
Anyone involved with your donor campaign: some combination of board, staff, and volunteers

Setting
A space large enough to accommodate several small groups of three to five each

Materials
- Flip chart paper and markers
- Paper and pens

FACILITATING THE EXERCISE

1. Ask your board and colleagues to form small groups of three to five to discuss the following: "Imagine you're opening the mail in our office and pull out a donation from an envelope. How large an amount does it need to be to get your attention?"

   Here's one shortcut for determining this number: what size gift would land a donor in the top 10 percent of your donor pool? Indeed, we suggest you calculate this amount in advance and share it with the group after they've come up with their own answers to this question.

2. Give the group a few minutes to identify an amount, then ask them to discuss the following: "How should we respond to gifts of that size so donors feel appreciated —and want to give again?" Encourage your colleagues to talk about thanking and appreciation but also ways to more deeply involve supporters in the work of the organization. After five to ten minutes, reconvene the large group to debrief their responses and record them on a flip chart.

3. Choose a number generated by one of the groups—a good number would be $250 or $500, but you could go higher—and give the following instructions: "We've chosen $____ as a significant gift. Write down anyone you know, including any current supporters, who you believe might be able to give that amount. If it would be helpful, feel free to look at the contact list in your smartphone or other device."

4. Give everyone a few minutes to work on this task. Some will struggle because the amount will feel large to them.

5. After a few minutes, ask for the group's attention and provide a new set of instructions by dividing the amount by twelve. Talk about monthly installments. Here's an example:

   "OK, $500 equals about $40 dollars per month. So please write down the name of anyone you know who might be able to give $40 per month. Here's one way to think about this: What would someone have to give up to afford this monthly gift? For example, if you take two people to the movies and buy everyone popcorn, that's $40. A nice meal for two? More than $40. How much does someone pay each month for their morning lattes? So let's assume that $40 per month is affordable for a wide range of people. Please add names of people who might contribute at that level if they chose to do so." Give the group another five to ten minutes to work on their lists.

6. To debrief this exercise, ask the following questions:

   - What did it feel like trying to generate a list of potential major donors?
   - Did dividing the total into monthly increments help you think differently about who might be a major donor?
   - Did the monthly giving option make you think differently about your own giving? If so, how?
   - How might we apply what we've learned here?

7. Collect the lists now or suggest a way to collect them later, after people have had more time to add more names and contact information.

TRAINING TIP Don't rush this exercise—especially the parts where people are sitting quietly, thinking through the names of people they know. Once they start, one name will trigger another and the list will grow, but it may take a while for people to get traction.

The VIP Prospect Game

Gail Perry of Fired Up Fundraising designed this exercise to help board members do what we always hope they'll do: identify and share the names of major gift prospects. Gail stresses the fun in fundraising; as she famously says, "When in doubt, throw a party." And while this exercise won't be mistaken for a party, it does feel a little like a game.

We appreciate the idea of having board members focus on identifying people who can "catapult" their organization to the next level. For most people, talking about moving to the next level, organizationally speaking, is a lot less daunting than talking about money.

Why Do This Exercise?
The more intentional you are about identifying and building relationships, the more successful your fundraising will be

Use This Exercise When
Your organization has plateaued in terms of money and effectiveness, and you need a spark to move to the next level

Time Required
15 minutes

Audience
Anyone involved with your fundraising campaign: some combination of board, staff, and volunteers

Setting
Anywhere you gather to work on your campaign plan and train your participants—preferably with people sitting in a circle or around a table

Materials
Paper and pens

FACILITATING THE EXERCISE

1. Begin with the following instructions:

    "Take a piece of paper and a pen. You will NOT be asked to turn in the paper at the end of the exercise.

    "See if you can identify ten individuals or organizations whose support could catapult our organization to a new level of prominence and effectiveness. The people you name can be current supporters, former donors, or new prospects.

"They must be people our organization could realistically approach, rather than famous wealthy strangers who live elsewhere."

2. Stand back quietly and let them work. You will see thoughtful looks as they write.

3. When you sense that most people have stopped writing, ask everyone to turn to a partner and discuss one name on their list. What do they know about that person? Why do they think that person's support could transform your organization?

4. Reconvene the full group. To debrief this exercise, ask the following questions:

   - Can you imagine "catapulting" our organization to the next level? What might that look like? What are the opportunities and risks associated with doing this?
   - What were the common qualities of the people or organizations on your list?
   - If we haven't approached these people in the past, why not? What's been stopping us?

5. Remember, don't ask people to turn in their lists. You can, however, end the activity by asking if anyone would be willing to serve on a VIP Prospect Working Group to help create a viable list of prospects.

We thank our colleague Gail Perry for sharing this exercise.

TRAINING TIP Sometimes a simple but powerful word or metaphor will help people think differently. In this case, the metaphor of a catapult conveys a major change in your organization. When you ask people to stop thinking about current circumstances and turn their attention to what might be, they start to envision more ambitious opportunities.

Power Mapping: Who Are the Movers and Shakers?

Most board members believe that none of their friends have money or influence, and they don't know how to identify influential people.

Well, it turns out they know a lot more about their communities than they realize but have never thought about power and influence in a concerted, strategic fashion. This exercise shows them how.

This activity works best for organizations in small to mid-size towns or cities. Really large cities like New York or Chicago have more complex power structures that can be more difficult, though not impossible, to map in this way.

Why Do This Exercise? To map a network of existing relationships to benefit your fundraising	**Audience** Anyone involved with your fundraising campaign: some combination of board, staff, and volunteers
Use This Exercise When You are getting ready for a capital campaign or some other significant fundraising effort	**Setting** A room with tables, chairs, and enough wall space to post at least ten flip chart pages
Time Required 30-45 minutes	**Materials** • Lots of flip chart paper • One marker for each person • Tape

FACILITATING THE EXERCISE

1. In advance, you will need to collect donor lists that appear in annual reports, newsletters, and programs from prominent local or regional nonprofits. For example, obtain a copy of the United Way annual report, an art museum newsletter, the local university alumni magazine, a program from a major performing arts organization, the e-newsletter from a regional conservation organization, and so forth. Also visit nonprofit websites and

look for donor lists. Ask board members to help collect these documents before you meet. You don't need copies for everyone, but it might be helpful to photocopy two or three of each.

2. Post at least ten blank flip chart pages around the room and set up an easel with flip chart paper at the front.

3. Pass around copies of the documents you've collected from other nonprofits. These can be referenced throughout the exercise to generate names.

4. Using the flip chart to track the group's responses, ask the participants to create a list of prominent entities in your community. Though every community is a bit different, the standard list includes major employers, government, news media, the local hospital, established nonprofits, banks, colleges and universities, the chamber of commerce, professional sports teams, civic and service clubs, large religious institutions.

5. Then ask for names of influential people who may not be affiliated with any of those institutions; add them to the list. Examples might include the former mayor, a well-known local author, a major landowner, or the high school principal.

6. Review everything you've written on the flip chart, looking for ways to combine or simplify the items on the list.

7. Write one institution on each of the pages posted around the room. The final list of unaffiliated individuals (if you have any) can be clustered on the last sheet.

8. Go from page to page, asking for the names of people who serve as trustees or senior staff within these institutions or are affiliated with them in some other way. Find out if anyone in the room knows these people, or knows someone who knows them. Write this information, adding the initials of the person who volunteered the name. Continue around the room until all the pages are full.

    Variation: Hand out markers and ask your colleagues to write the names themselves. This is a quicker and more energetic process, but it may yield less information than a facilitator repeatedly asking the group, "Come on, who *else* do we know?"

9. When the flip chart pages are complete, pass out markers and ask each participant to put a star by the name of three people he or she thinks would be

great additions to your organization as board members, committee members, or donors. Emphasize that they should choose people you can reach through an existing relationship, as indicated in the notes near each name.

10. Debrief the exercise by asking some combination of the following questions:

   • How does it feel to see all of the relationships we already have?
   • Were you surprised to see any of these connections or relationships? If so, which ones?
   • If our goal is to connect these people more strongly to our organization, where should we focus our efforts?
   • How do we use this information? What are our next steps?

After the meeting, create a spreadsheet from the information gathered. Distribute it to the participants for additions or corrections.

TRAINING TIP Some work is best accomplished individually, while other tasks are best done in groups. Generating lists of names definitely works better in groups, where one suggestion seems to spin off another.

Two simple tricks will help jump-start any group. First, prepare a few individuals in advance (in the old days, we called these people plants or ringers) to kick off the discussion. Second, never disrespect anyone by criticizing his or her suggestion. Write it on the flip chart with all the others. In the process of selecting and implementing the group's best ideas, the most impractical options will be weeded out.

Rating Your Prospects (Pizza and Beer)

If you're organizing a face-to-face fundraising campaign, eventually you have to sit down together as a team to discuss assignments. This exercise will help you prioritize potential donors for personal solicitations. By the end of the meeting, most prospects will be assigned to specific askers—presumably the people participating in the meeting.

As you'll read below, you can also use this moment to test the feasibility of your campaign goal. If you don't have enough prospects (or enough askers to engage those prospects) you're unlikely to meet your target. In that case, you need to identify more prospects, more askers, or both—or lower your goal.

Why Do This Exercise?
Before launching a major gifts campaign, you need to decide who will ask whom and how much to ask for

Use This Exercise When
You are ready to test the reality of your fundraising goal and start making assignments

Time Required
About 2 hours. It can take more or less time, depending on the number of names to be discussed and the skill of the facilitator in keeping everyone on task—because this exercise can easily degenerate into idle gossip and speculation

Audience
The leadership team for your fundraising campaign: some combination of board, staff, and volunteers. This exercise can be done with as few as three participants and as many as a dozen. In general, the more involved, the more productive the process

Setting
A private room with enough wall space to hang five or six sheets of flip chart paper. Because you will be discussing donor names and ask amounts, privacy is important

Materials
- Flip chart paper and markers
- A gift chart for your campaign; see Building a Gift Chart on page 88
- Prospect lists developed through the ABCs of Identifying Prospects on page 106
- A list of *current donors* who give at one of the gift chart levels or might be able to contribute at one of those levels. Remember, donors will typically give five to ten times more money in person than they'll send through the mail.
- Bonus item: published donor lists from peer nonprofits that operate in your area. You can find them in nonprofit newsletters, annual reports, event programs, and websites. These lists are often segmented by gift size, which

will give you some sense of a prospect's giving potential. (It's worth noting that top-tier gifts go to organizations that meaningfully engage their donors and prospects, rather than those that only contact donors to ask for money.)

- Food and beverages for the participants.

FACILITATING THE EXERCISE

A client calls this the "pizza and beer exercise" to highlight its informality: sitting around with colleagues, talking about people you know, estimating how much money to ask them for, and figuring out who will do the asking. Alcohol is optional; food, probably not. Given the nature of the work, everyone must swear the confidentiality oath: whatever is discussed in this meeting must remain confidential—which might be an argument against serving alcohol.

1. Post several sheets of flip chart paper on the wall. At the top of each page, write an amount from each line of your gift chart. For example, one sheet might be marked $500, the next $1,000, the next $2,500, and so on.

2. Hand out your gift chart, prospect lists, and published donor lists from peer nonprofits. Give everyone a few minutes to read through the names and ask any questions; don't spend too much time (yet) discussing specific prospects.

3. Start with your highest gift level; for example, "Let's begin with $25,000. You've read through the lists —who might be able to give a $25,000 donation?" This involves a certain amount of guesswork, but the collective wisdom of the group tends to keep the numbers realistic. ("Boy, I'd have to disagree about Jerry. I think he's more of a $5,000 prospect.") If you've collected lists from other groups, you can always check your guesses against a particular donor's gifts to peer organizations.

   Keep pushing participants to add more names: "Is there anyone else we could approach for a gift that size?" Once you've written all the names for that amount, move down through the levels, writing names on the relevant pieces of flip chart paper. You may find yourself jumping from chart to chart as people suggest prospects.

4. After recording all the names, review the list a second time and make assignments. "Ed, you mentioned Sandy Yang. Are you willing to be the solicitor? Great—who would like to help Ed with that one?" As a general

rule, pairing up solicitors—usually a staff member plus a trustee—is a good strategy but not essential.

Because this is a brainstorm—and because people are squeamish about fundraising—not all prospects will be assigned. That's okay. The following step will make sure you end the exercise with appropriate expectations.

5. Finally, it's time to reality-test your campaign goal. A simple way to do this is to add up the cash value of all *assigned* gift amounts—in other words, any prospects with a solicitor assigned. If you have ten assigned prospects on the $1,000 page, write $10,000 on the bottom of the sheet. Repeat this on every page, then add the total from all pages and *divide by two*. This is your feasible number.

   By dividing the total by two, you're accounting for solicitors who don't follow through, donors who choose not to meet, and those who give less than anticipated.

   By the end of the meeting, you should have a good sense of whether your goal is achievable. If it's not, you have several options: identify more prospects, identify more askers who will accept assignments, lower your goal, or start asking the people you've identified and see what happens.

6. To debrief this exercise, ask the following questions:

   • How is everyone feeling about our goal? Is it achievable? Why or why not?
   • To the best of our knowledge, are these donors ready to be asked? If not, what additional cultivation steps can we start now?
   • Did anything take place during this exercise that surprised or inspired you?

> **TRAINING TIP** This exercise can easily degenerate into idle gossip, so keep everyone on task. One way to achieve this is to set a time limit for each prospect and recruit a timekeeper: "We're going to limit ourselves to 30 seconds per name. Marvin, would you be willing to help by keeping track of the time?"

PART 6

Asking for the Gift

Many of us learned as children that talking about money—and even worse, asking for it—is something we shouldn't do. It's no wonder that asking makes people nervous. You've probably heard board members and other volunteers say, "I'm just not able to ask for money," or "I'll help in any way, just don't make me ask."

Unfortunately, you're not likely to raise much money if you don't meet with your best supporters and ask for their support. When surveyed, the number one reason cited by donors for not giving is that they haven't been asked.

Hence, the conundrum: the most effective way to raise money is to look someone in the eye and ask for it. The scariest way to raise money is to look someone in the eye and ask for it. In other words, the strategy that works best is the one we most consciously avoid.

How do we address this challenge? Training! Good training increases comfort, skill, and confidence. Give people a chance to practice in safe and engaging ways, and they'll be more willing to go out and ask.

This chapter's hands-on exercises are all about "the ask." Teach them to your board members and volunteers, encourage them to practice with each other, and watch what happens.

Active Listening: What Did You Hear?

00:15

Listening may be the most important skill in face-to-face fundraising. This exercise reminds solicitors who tend to talk too much (in other words, most of us) about the value of active listening. To quote a training manual for hospice volunteers, "We listen, waiting to impose on the speaker a detailed account of our own personal experience"—which is obviously a poor model for building respectful relationships. This exercise will help you create a better model.

Why Do This Exercise?
To help your trainees focus less on the pitch—what they say about your organization—and focus more on the donor's needs and interests

Use This Exercise When
You're preparing to meet with donors and you want to strengthen your listening skills

Time Required
10-15 minutes

Audience
Anyone who plans to conduct meetings with donors

Setting
A quiet room large enough for people to pair up, talk, and hear each other

Materials
• Stopwatch or timer
• Bell or whistle

FACILITATING THE EXERCISE

1. Ask participants to pair up, preferably with someone they don't know well.

2. One member of the pair says to the other, "Tell me a story—the more specific, the better—about your favorite relative. Why is this person your favorite? Why is this story important to you?" The speaker can take up to two minutes to answer. The listener should listen without taking notes.

3. After two minutes, ring the bell. The listener then repeats the story in his or her own words. The goal is not to remember the story word for word, but rather to accurately paraphrase it.

4. The speaker provides feedback to the listener: you remembered this part well, here's something you might have missed.

5. After a minute or two, ask the teams to switch roles and repeat the exercise.

6. Reconvene the full group. Debrief the exercise by asking the following questions.

    - What did you learn?
    - While your partner was speaking, what did you find yourself doing *other than* listening? How might you address that tendency in the future?
    - If you were asked to do this exercise again, what would you do differently? Why? How?
    - What are three things you can do when you visit a donor to make sure you really listen?

TRAINING TIP As with many role plays, it helps to model what you want in front of the group before asking everyone to participate. In this case, recruit someone to tell you a story about a favorite relative, then follow the instructions above.

Ask Good Questions, Become a Better Listener

This exercise reminds us that the most effective communicators use open-ended questions to stimulate conversation. With this simple, hands-on activity, board members will learn the power of asking questions that create active dialogue—which will make them better ambassadors and advocates for your work.

Why Do This Exercise?
Skilled fundraisers are good at asking questions; this exercise reminds us how and why

Use This Exercise When
Your board members keep coming back to "the pitch" or the "elevator speech," rather than focusing on how to better engage donors and learn about their needs and interests

Time Required
20-30 minutes

Audience
Anyone who plans to conduct meetings with donors

Setting
A room large enough to accommodate your group sitting in chairs back to back, and quiet enough for people to hear each other

Materials
- Stopwatch or timer
- Bell or whistle
- Flip chart paper and markers
- Paper and pencils with erasers
- Handouts (pages 129-131)

FACILITATING THE EXERCISE

1. Prior to the session, write the following on a flip chart page:

Close-ended questions
- Result in "yes" or "no" answers
- Often start with the words "is," "do," or "does"

Open-ended questions
- Generate discussion
- Often start with the words "what" or "how" or "tell me about ..."

2. Before the session, make enough photocopies of the three images on pages 129-131 so that each pair will have one full set. It's important that the participants *not see these handouts in advance.*

3. Introduce the exercise by telling people you want to conduct an experiment about different ways of communicating. Using the flip chart page you prepared in advance, briefly describe the difference between close- and open-ended questions. Open-ended questions lead naturally to discussion, while close-ended questions lead to "yes" or "no" answers. Many people are familiar with this concept, but a brief description will ensure that everyone understands the distinction. You can offer simple examples like "Have you ever heard of our organization?" (close-ended) vs. "*What have you heard about our organization?*" (open-ended).

   Explain that the exercise is done in pairs and includes three two-minute rounds. They will stay in the same pairs for all three rounds but will switch roles after each round.

4. Distribute a pad and pencil (with an eraser) to each participant. For this exercise, blank paper works better than lined. Ask the group members to pair up and turn their chairs back to back so they can't see what their partners see.

5. Hand out the first image (page 129) to one person in each pair, instructing them not to show it to their partners. Tell them that when you say, "Go," the person with the handout will have two minutes to describe the illustration in a way that will enable the other person to reproduce it on their blank page. The person who is drawing may not ask any questions or turn to look at the printed image. Ring the bell after two minutes and ask the participants to put the printed illustration and the drawing aside.

6. Hand out the second image (page 130) to the person who drew during the first round. Once again, the person with the printed image will describe it, and his or her partner will attempt to draw it accurately. This time, however, the person who is drawing can ask close-ended questions and their partner can respond—but only using the words "yes" or "no." For example, the drawer might ask, "Is the circle in the middle of the page?" But he or she may not ask, "Where on the page is the circle?" After two minutes, ring the bell again and ask each pair to put their drawings aside.

7. Have them switch roles one more time and distribute the third figure (page 131). The goal is the same, but this time the person drawing the

picture may ask any sort of question—open- or close-ended—and his or her partner may answer. As before, give them two minutes to complete the drawing.

8. When everyone is done, ask the teams to compare all three drawings with the original illustrations and discuss the differences with their teammate. Give them about two to three minutes for this conversation.

9. To debrief this exercise, ask some combination of the following questions:

   - When you compare the drawings, did you see a progression from round to round? What happened?
   - How did your experience change as you could ask and answer more questions?
   - What did you learn that you might apply in your role as a fundraiser?

10. To conclude the exercise, take a few minutes to brainstorm specific open-ended questions you might ask donors and prospects. For example, "You've contributed for several years now, and we appreciate your generosity. Why is our work meaningful to you?"

We thank our colleague Anne Loehr for sharing this exercise.

TRAINING TIP In setting up this exercise (or any other in this book), be careful not to bury people under too many details. The best way to present an exercise is to a provide a simple step-by-step description, then give participants an opportunity to ask questions before diving in.

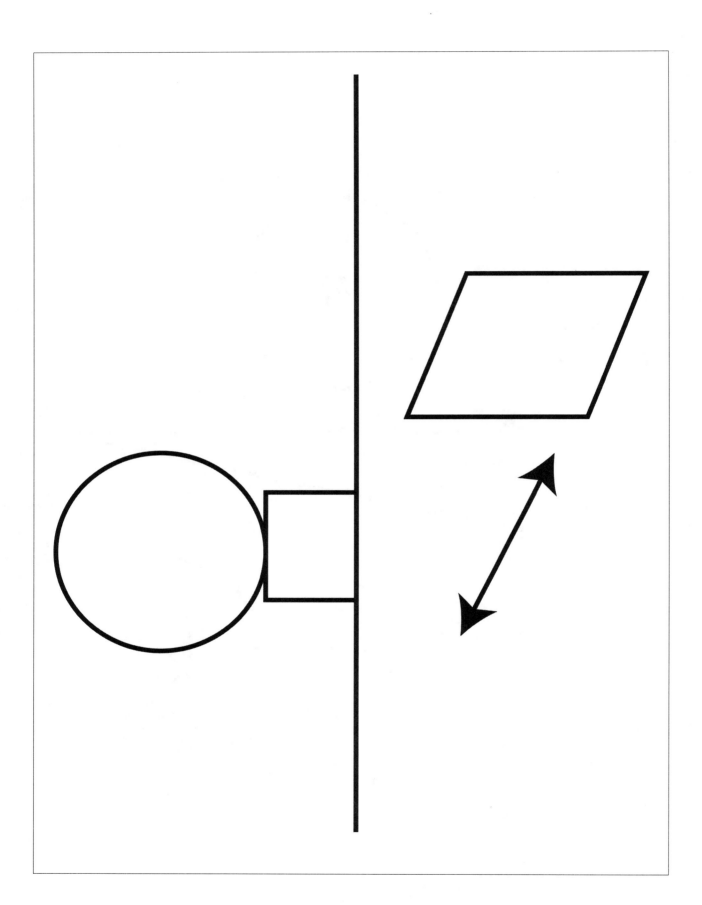

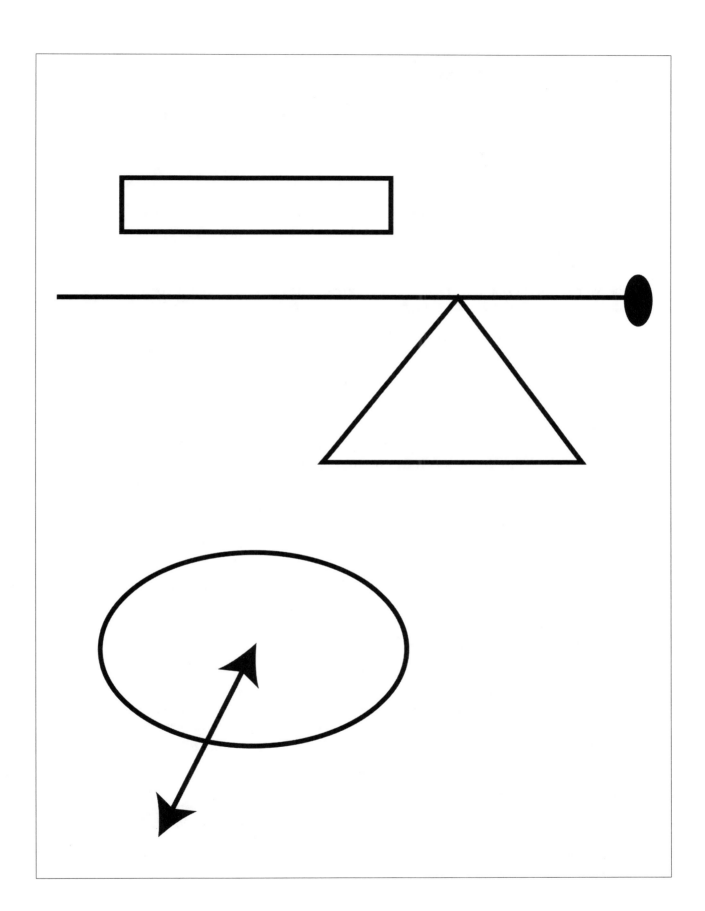

Shall We Meet?
Overcoming Objections by Phone

The biggest gifts are raised in person, and most donor meetings are scheduled by telephone. Because phoning can be the most challenging step in major gifts fundraising, people tend to avoid the phone or give up too easily.

It's worth noting that email can also be a great scheduling tool, but it comes with certain limitations. Email does a lousy job of conveying tone of voice, it's harder to counter objections, and some donors don't respond to email. As every experienced solicitor learns, sooner or later you have to pick up the telephone.

It's impossible to overemphasize the value of telephone role plays like the following. Lacking skills or confidence, your callers will run into a simple objection—"Can't talk now, I'm cooking dinner"—and respond with a pathetic, "Uh, okay," and hang up the phone. If this becomes a pattern, you'll burn through your list, schedule very few meetings, and raise far less money than you could.

This exercise requires some preparation and takes a little longer, but it's guaranteed to build everyone's skills and courage.

Why Do This Exercise?
To develop a kind of "verbal muscle memory" by practicing your responses—again and again—to a series of common objections

Use This Exercise When
People are getting ready to pick up the phone and call donors for appointments

Time Required
90 minutes for the exercise, plus 10 minutes in advance to set up the room

Audience
The leadership team for your fundraising campaign: some combination of board, staff, and volunteers. This exercise can be done with as few as four and as many as twenty.

Setting
A large room with lots of blank wall space for hanging flip chart paper, plus enough room for participants to move around

Materials
- Bell or whistle
- Flip chart paper and markers
- Enough chairs for all participants
- Handout: Do I Hear Any Objections? Responses to Common Put-Offs (pages 135-136)

FACILITATING THE EXERCISE

1. Before you begin, post 8 to 10 pieces of flip chart paper around the room as far away from each other as possible. Post them at eye level so people can write comfortably. You will also need a flip chart easel with paper at the front of the room.

2. Once everyone has gathered around the easel, ask the participants, "If we call people and ask for a meeting, and our goal for this meeting is to ask for a gift, what objections are they likely to offer?" As the participants suggest objections, write them on the easel pad. For example, "I don't have time to talk," or "Why do we need to meet? Can't I just send you a check?" or "I usually talk with my spouse before making a gift." For more ideas, see Do I Hear Any Objections? on pages 135-136.

3. Ask the group to help you select the eight to ten most common objections from the list. Walk around the room and write one per page on the flip chart paper you posted earlier.

4. Hand out markers and ask everyone to circle the room, writing their best responses to each particular objection. For example, on the page titled, "My spouse and I make donations together," one person might write, "Can we schedule a time for the three of us to meet together?" This is in essence a problem-solving exercise, so encourage participants to be creative with their answers.

5. Once the responses are complete, ask everyone to circle the room again and review all the responses.

6. Place two chairs in front of each piece of paper. Place them *back to back*, because this exercise simulates a phone call and you can't see your partner. Ask the participants to pair up and sit down together in front of an objection page. One places the call; the other offers the same objection *over and over*, so the caller can try out different responses. The goal is to respond effectively and almost automatically by using several repetitions of the same answer. For example,

    Donor: "I don't have time to talk now."
    Asker: "Sorry to bother you. When would be a better time to call?"

    Donor: "I don't have time to talk now."
    Asker: "Uh, is there a time that would be more convenient?"

Donor:	"I don't have time to talk now."
Asker:	"I would be happy to call back. When shall I call again?"
Donor:	(Pause) "Those are all good responses. Pick one and let's do it a few more times. Ready? I don't have time to talk now."
Asker:	"Sorry to bother you. When would be a better time to call?"
Donor:	"I don't have time to talk now."
Asker:	"Sorry to bother you. When would be a better time to call?"

And so on.

Repetition is the point of this exercise. Most people will try out different phrases and responses until they find an answer that feels comfortable. Once selected, repeating that answer multiple times helps to hard wire it into the brain.

7. After about three minutes—ninety seconds for each person in a pair to practice—ring the bell. All pairs rotate to a new station, practicing back and forth using the new objection. After another three minutes ring the bell again. The exercise continues until all pairs have rotated to at least five different stations and practiced their responses to those objections. If you sense enough energy in the room, the pairs can continue the rotation until they have practiced responses to all the posted objections.

8. To debrief the exercise, reconvene the group and ask the following questions:

   - Which objection was hardest for you to counter—and how did you deal with it?
   - As you went from objection to objection, how did the exercise change? What did you learn from one that you could apply to responding to others?
   - If someone calls you—in real life—to request a meeting, will you respond differently because of the work you just completed? How?

TRAINING TIP Because of the logistics involved and the time it takes, this is a relatively complex exercise. A simpler version is to ask everyone to choose a phone partner, schedule a call, and practice with each other on actual telephones. Indeed, you could ask everyone to bring their cell phones to the training, pair up, and then call each other from different corners of the same room.

Do I Hear Any Objections?

RESPONSES TO COMMON PUT-OFFS

The Three Rules of Telephone Appointment Making

1. Whatever the objection, take it literally. Rather than making assumptions about what other people mean, take them at their word. The corollary is this: if they say no—a clear, explicit no—you have to honor that.

2. Assume success. Don't say, "Do you want to meet?" Ask, "When do you want to meet?" This is a subtle distinction, but it makes a big difference. Or you might propose one of two specific dates. "How about Wednesday afternoon or Friday morning first thing?"

3. Keep bringing it back to your agenda. "When do you want to meet?"

Sooner or later you'll have this experience. After a few words of explanation—"Hi Leroy, this is Andy. I'm following up on the letter I sent about our fall fundraising campaign"—the person on the other end of the phone will say, "Sure, I'd love to get together. When's a good time for you?" Until that day, however, you must learn to respond to the most common objections. *We don't mean to imply that this is one conversation and you have to handle five or six consecutive put-offs.* The general rule, however, is that you should respond to at least three before giving up.

Objection: "I don't have time to talk right now."
Response: "When would be a good time to call?"

Objection: "You sent me a letter? What letter?" (Or alternatively, "There's a pile of mail on the kitchen table—bills and such—and I've been avoiding it.")
Response: "Well, let me tell you about the letter."

Objection: "I don't really have the time to meet. Can't we just do this over the phone?"
Response: "That's up to you. The meeting takes about twenty minutes, and I'll make it as convenient as possible—I can come to your home or office, whatever works for you. This just works better if we meet face to face. But if you'd prefer, we can talk about it now."

Objection: "Why me? I don't give that much."
Response: "We're meeting with a handful of our most loyal supporters before we roll out the campaign to a larger group of donors. Based on your past support, we wanted to talk with you early and get your feedback."

Objection: "I can't afford the amount you're asking for."
Response: "The amount is completely up to you. Let's sit down together, discuss it, and then you'll decide."

Objection: "You know, I generally make charitable decisions with my spouse/partner/financial advisor/eight-year-old child/psychic friend."
Response: "Is it appropriate for the three of us to sit down together? If so, when would be a good time? If not, how can I help you to have that discussion—maybe the two of us could meet first?"

Objection: "You know, I support so many other groups and I'm tapped out for this year."
Response: "I know the feeling. Tell you what—let's take the money off the table. I'd still like to meet with you because A) I'd like to thank you for your generous support last year, and B) when you're budgeting for next year, perhaps you could remember us then. So let's assume you won't be giving now—I hear that. But I'd still like to meet. When would be a good time?"

Objection: "I gave because of your work on _____, but I don't like the position you've taken on _____."
Response: "You know, I'd like to hear more about your concerns. Frankly, I don't like everything the organization does, but overall I believe the mission and the work are important. Let's get together and talk about it; then you can decide. If you choose not to give, I certainly respect that. When would be a good time to meet?"

Objection: "We're down to one income and we don't have the money."
Response: "I'm sorry to hear that. Is there some other way you'd like to be involved in our work?"

Objection: "This is just not a priority right now."
Response: "Well, your past support has meant a lot to us. Shall we keep you on the mailing list? Is it appropriate to contact you again in the future?"

You're probably thinking, "What's wrong with these people? Can't they take 'no' for an answer?" Our response: when people say no—*"We don't have the money"* or *"This is not a priority right now"*—we hear them say no. But when they say, *"That's more than I can afford,"* or *"I have to talk with my spouse first,"* that doesn't mean that they don't want to give—it means that they want to choose the amount, or would prefer to consult with someone else before making a decision.

As you pick up the phone to make appointments, always remember that the relationship trumps the money—and the best way to build relationships is face to face. In deciding how hard to push for a meeting, find your own comfort level. If the suggestions above seem a bit too assertive for your taste, back off a little. Strive for a balance between assertiveness and humility, between boldness and fear. If you give in to the fear—if you backpedal at the first objection—you do a disservice to yourself, your group, and your donors. Be bold and watch what happens.

Face-to-Face Fundraising: Structuring the Meeting

The novice solicitor often wonders, "What do I say to the donor? How does the conversation actually work? When do I ask for the money?" By providing a step-by-step process for the donor meeting, this exercise addresses those questions.

This activity is designed to precede the Trio Ask exercise on page 148, as a way of preparing everyone for that role play. It's different from most activities in this book: a bit more lecture, a little less group participation. This is why we encourage you to pair it with the Trio Ask. Taken together, these two exercises will markedly increase the comfort, skill, and confidence of your askers.

Why Do This Exercise?
When your solicitors understand that donor meetings follow a clear sequence, they'll be less nervous and more effective

Use This Exercise When
You're getting ready to meet with donors

Time Required
30 minutes

Audience
Anyone who plans to conduct meetings with donors

Setting
A space large enough to accommodate several small groups of three to five each

Materials
- Flip chart paper and markers
- Handout: Face-to-Face Fundraising: Structuring the Meeting (pages 140-141)

FACILITATING THE EXERCISE

1. In advance, prepare a flip chart page summarizing the steps in the meeting. You'll find them in bold type below. Make photocopies of the handout on pages 140-141.

2. When your group gathers, share copies of the handout and talk your colleagues through the steps of the donor visit as follows:

a) **Briefly build rapport** with the prospect by discussing any mutual interests, friends, activities.

Question for the group: How much time should we spend on chitchat?
Answer: It depends on the situation. Some people want to discuss the organization and their donation; others want to tell you about their grandchildren. Be sensitive and adaptable.

b) **State your goals for the meeting**, which include learning more about the donor's interests, providing some "inside information" on your work, and asking for financial support.

Question for the group: Why is this a good strategy?
Answer: So everyone has the same expectations about why you're sitting down together. As the solicitor, it also signals that you're running (or at least facilitating) the meeting.

c) **Uncover the prospect's needs and interests.** Why does he or she care about your issue or programs?

Question for the group: What are some questions we could ask prospective donors to learn more about their connection to our work?
Answer: The answer will depend largely on your mission, but good basic questions would be "Why have you supported us in the past? What is it about our work that interests you?"

d) **Make a brief presentation** about your work and the donor's impact through his or her support, allowing the donor to participate.

Question for the group: What are two or three meaningful things about our work we could share with supporters?
Answer: Again, this depends on your mission, but don't limit yourself to facts and data—it's helpful to tell stories, too. For example, talk about your theater program for kids, citing a specific anecdote. Or how your advocacy led to a change in state law that protects clean water. Or tell a story about a family that has a new home, thanks to your housing program. The more specific, the better.

e) **Ask for the gift**, naming a specific amount or a range (or handing the prospect a copy of the gift chart; see samples on pages 90-91). After asking, keep quiet and wait for the prospect to respond.

Question for the group: What language can we use when we ask?
Answer: For ideas, see Closing the Gift on page 145.

f) **Deal with any concerns or objections.**

Question for the group: What are one or two objections we might hear—and how do we address them?
Answer: Obviously, the responses will depend on the objections. It might be helpful to pause your presentation, ask the group to pick one or two objections and work through their responses, preferably in pairs or groups of three.

g) **Close the meeting** by restating and clarifying any agreements or next steps.

Question for the group: What problems might we run into if we leave the meeting without a clear understanding of next steps?
Answer: Donors may hint or imply what they're going to do, rather than saying, "I'll give you $1,000 within the next two weeks." It's helpful to ensure everyone is clear about what transpired during the meeting and who's responsible for the next steps. A good follow-up exercise is After the Yes: Questions You Can Ask Donors on page 162.

h) **Report the results** to fundraising staff or the campaign chair.

Question for the group: What problems could happen if you don't contact the office after the meeting?
Answer: Oh, let us count the ways: late thank you notes, unclear follow-up instructions, inaccurate data in the database, poor follow-through with donors, and missed opportunities.

3. To debrief the exercise, ask the following questions:

- What's one aspect of the donor meeting you now understand more clearly? Why?
- What's one portion of the donor meeting you feel you need to practice?
- Is any of this likely to change your own behavior? If so, why? How?

TRAINING TIP Encourage questions and do your best to answer them. If you're stumped, use the old trainer trick: kick it back to the group and rely on their collective wisdom. "Juanita," you say, "that's a great question. Who has a good answer?"

Face-to-Face Fundraising:

STRUCTURING THE MEETING

1. **Build rapport.** Chat a little. Start with topics having no bearing on your organization or fundraising campaign. "How's your job? What are your kids doing these days? I notice you've got your garden in; what are you growing this year?" Don't spend a lot of time on idle chatter—the meeting could get away from you—but it's good manners to ease into the topic at hand.

2. **State your goals for the meeting.** This step is optional but recommended. You might say, "Margarita, I've come today with three things on my mind. One, I'm here to tell you about our work. Two, I want to learn more about you and your interests. Three, it's my responsibility to ask for your financial support. To tell you the truth, I'd like to know why you're interested in our organization, so let's start there." This provides a clean segue into the next item.

3. **Uncover the person's needs and interests.** Find out why he or she cares about your work. For a donor, the questions might be, "You gave us $500 last year, which is a big gift. Why did you do it? Why do you care about this issue?" When talking with a prospect who is considering a first gift, perhaps you can ask, "What's your experience with our work? Why does it interest you?" Initiate a dialogue by asking questions.

4. **Present your organization: your goals, programs, and what the donor's gift could accomplish.** Provide "inside information." Tell stories. Where relevant, cite statistics. Keep it brief; don't overwhelm the person by reciting your 14-point strategic plan. If you have visuals that tell your story—maps, graphs, photos, charts, or site plans—this is an opportunity to use them. Encourage questions.

5. **Ask for the gift.** Look the donor directly in the eye. Be clear, explicit, and straightforward. "Sally, as I mentioned in the letter, would you consider a gift of $1,000 to support our work? Your gift would have a huge impact in the community. What do you say?" As an alternative, "As I mentioned in the letter, we're seeking gifts of between $500 and $5,000 toward a goal of $50,000. I appreciate that this is a wide range—the amount is up to you. Please give as generously as you can."

   Once you've asked for the gift, wait—*keep your mouth closed*. Don't make excuses or start to backpedal before the donor has a chance to respond. Just sit quietly and wait.

6. **Deal with any objections.** Some of the objections you answered by phone are likely to come up again now. Think in advance about these objections and how you might respond. For example, if the person says, "You're asking for more than I can afford," you can reply, "The amount is up to you. I hope you will give as generously as possible. What do you think you could afford?" In response to, "I'm unable to give right now," you could say, "Another option is to make a pledge now and pay later. If that works for you, it works for us." Most of these responses are nothing more than common sense, so:

   - Take a breath
   - Ask yourself, "What's the logical response to this concern?"
   - Respond accordingly

7. **Close the meeting.** Restate any agreements you've made so both parties leave with the same expectations. Once again, be clear, explicit, and straightforward.

8. **Report your results** to the fundraising staff or campaign chair to ensure appropriate follow-up with the donor.

Trust Your Instincts:
Six Quick Asks ☑ 00:30

This activity is a great warm-up for other, more complex role plays. You can even use it as a warm-up before a meeting with a real donor. It'll help you learn to think on your feet, which is a key skill for fundraisers. Facilitators love it because it brings instant energy to the room and it's simple to organize.

Why Do This Exercise?
Because sooner or later you will have to answer the question "Why should I give?"

Use This Exercise When
You are preparing people for face-to-face solicitations

Time Required
20-30 minutes

Audience
Anyone involved with your fundraising campaign: some combination of board, staff, and volunteers—especially those who are preparing for visits with donors

Setting
A quiet room large enough for people to pair up, talk, and hear each other

Materials
None

FACILITATING THE EXERCISE

1. First model the exercise. Recruit a partner to join you at the front of the room. Explain that your partner's job is to ask you the question "Why should I give?" six times in a row. Your job, in modeling the exercise, is to come up with six different answers, customized to address what you know about your partner. For example,

   "Why should I give?"
   "Sally, our organization sustains the community programs your mother helped create. Your gift would be a great way to honor your family legacy."

   "Yes, but why should I give?"
   "Our group is one of the most effective in the city, and I know you like to invest in groups that use money wisely and achieve tangible results. That's why we're asking you to consider a gift."

"That's good, but why should I give?"

"Sally, you're one of our most dedicated volunteers—so you understand that volunteer labor isn't enough to get everything done. Your gift supports the staff and training that makes volunteers like you so productive and increases our impact."

(Continue with three more variations on "Why should I give?")

If you like, encourage your partner to incorporate a few common excuses into the questions. For example, "I already support several organizations—why should I give to yours?" or "I don't have much money at the moment—why should I give?" As you model the exercise, do your best to provide thoughtful responses to the questions.

2. When you complete your six responses, take a bow and enjoy the applause. Spend a few minutes on feedback from the group: what they observed, what worked, and what might be improved.

3. Provide the following instructions to your participants.

    a) Pair up; choose someone you don't work with very often. (If both board and staff are being trained together, suggest board-staff pairs.)

    b) Within each pair, decide who will be first to ask the questions and who will answer them.

    c) The person being solicited asks the question six times: Why should I give? Variations on this question are encouraged. If you're responding, do your best to come up with six different answers.

    d) Switch roles and repeat.

    e) Once you've completed the role play, take a few minutes to give each other feedback: What worked? What could we each do to make the case more effectively?

4. After the role play and feedback, reconvene the full group to debrief the exercise by asking some combination of the following questions:

    • What worked? What did you do well?
    • Who heard a good response to the question "Why should I give?" that you're willing to share?
    • What do the most effective responses have in common?

One reason this exercise is effective is that with each subsequent reply to the question "Why should I give?" solicitors tend to come up with deeper, more meaningful answers, because they use the easy ones first. These later responses tend to have greater impact.

We thank our colleagues at the Center for Progressive Leadership for sharing this exercise.

TRAINING TIP The success of this exercise depends, to some degree, on how well you model the answers at the start. If you require a lot of preparation, set aside time to practice in advance with a friend or colleague, or even in the mirror. Talk into a voice recorder. You don't have to be flawless, but you do need to be comfortable and authentic.

And if you're one of those people who prefers improvisation to preparation, this activity was made for you. Jump in and have fun with it.

Closing the Gift

Most of what we call fundraising takes place before or after you receive the gift: prospecting, cultivation, recognition, donor engagement, and so on. You can do all those things supremely well and still miss *the* essential step: sooner or later, you have to ask for the money. This exercise is designed to increase everyone's comfort by providing specific language, then giving you a chance to practice until you find the words that work best for you.

Why Do This Exercise?
To increase your comfort in asking for money, including requesting specific amounts

Use This Exercise When
You're preparing to meet with donors to ask for support. Given the time needed to schedule and conduct donor meetings, we strongly recommend face-to-face asks of at least $500 or ($40 per month) for grassroots organizations, and progressively larger minimum asks for larger nonprofits.

Time Required
30 minutes

Audience
Anyone who plans to meet with donors to solicit gifts

Setting
A quiet room large enough for participants to pair up, talk, and hear each other

Materials
- Flip chart paper and markers
- Sample gift charts (pages 90-91)
- Closing the Gift: Sample Scripts (page 147)

FACILITATING THE EXERCISE

1. Ask participants to pair up, preferably with someone they don't know well. Explain that the purpose of this exercise is to try out different ways of asking for a contribution. Ask each pair to come up with three different ways—specific language—to ask for a gift. You might offer an example or two from the handout Closing the Gift: Sample Scripts on page 147.

2. After about two minutes, reconvene the full group. Encourage each team to report its favorite one or two ways to ask, taking notes on the flip chart as they speak.

3. Distribute the handout Closing the Gift: Sample Scripts on page 147, and also the gift charts on pages 90-91. If you've already created a gift pyramid

for your campaign, use that instead of the samples in this book. Give participants a minute or two to read these materials, reminding them that the gift charts can be used as a solicitation tool when talking with donors.

4. Explain that the next portion of the exercise is a role play. Using a combination of the language developed so far in this exercise and the sample language in the handout, ask the partners to practice back and forth, testing out and combining several options until they find a few they are comfortable with.

    For example, the donor might ask, "How much are you giving?" and the solicitor would respond accordingly, picking language from the scripts and personalizing it. Or the donor could say, "What do you want me to do?" giving the asker the chance to try several responses.

    Note that some scripts include a dollar amount, while others leave the amount to the donor. Encourage your trainees to try some of each.

5. When the role play is complete—give the teams about ten minutes— debrief it by asking the full group some combination of these questions:

    - What were your favorite phrases? Why?
    - When you were playing the prospect—the one being asked for the gift—what language or approach worked best for you? Why?
    - Is it important to get the language right? Why or why not?
    - What is one unexpected thing you learned from this exercise?

TRAINING TIP Before starting this exercise, take a look at the Building a Gift Chart exercise on page 88. As you hand out copies of the sample gift charts for use during this exercise, you may need to review with the group how gift pyramids are created and why they're important.

Closing the Gift

SAMPLE SCRIPTS

- "Is there an amount you'd feel comfortable pledging today?"

- "As you know, I had three goals for this meeting: giving you an update on our work, learning more about your interests and concerns, and asking for your support. We've completed the first two. Are you ready to talk about a gift? Would you consider a donation of $___?"

- [Handing donor the gift chart and pointing out the low and high amounts] "We were hoping you would consider a gift of between $___ and $___. That would be really significant for our work. What do you say?"

- "As a board member, this organization is one of my top three charitable commitments. I believe you feel as strongly about the work as I do, so I hope you'll consider making it one of your top three."

- "During this campaign, we're talking with a handful of people who really understand our work and would be willing to make leadership gifts. Would you be able to pledge___?"

- [Handing donor the gift chart] "Here's our fundraising plan, showing the gifts we'll need to reach our goal and better serve our community. Please take a look, and I'd ask you to choose the amount that's right for you."

- "For this campaign, our family gave the biggest contribution we've ever given—and it felt good. What amount would feel good to you?"

- "I thought about how much I would feel comfortable giving, and then I decided to stretch myself a little. We're hoping you're inspired to give a 'stretch gift,' too. Would you consider a gift of $___?"

- [Handing donor the gift chart] "To be honest, I have no idea how much to ask you for. I don't want to insult you by asking for too much or too little. Please take a look at the chart and give me some guidance. How much should I ask for?"

Trio Ask

We know a skilled trainer who calls this "the Cadillac of role plays"—expansive and comfortable, but one requiring some energy to make it run. In addition to the solicitor and the prospect, it includes an observer who functions like a backseat driver ... but in a good way.

When training clients for donor meetings, we return to this exercise again and again because it provides the best preparation for what they're likely to experience during a real visit.

Before organizing this exercise, we strongly urge you to take your colleagues through Face-to-Face Fundraising: Structuring the Meeting on page 137.

Why Do This Exercise?
Because it provides the most specific, detailed preparation for conducting donor visits

Use This Exercise When
You have donor meetings scheduled ... soon!

Time Required
60 minutes

Audience
Anyone involved with your fundraising campaign who will participate in donor visits: some combination of board, staff, and volunteers

Setting
A quiet room that's large enough for your group to form triads and easily hear one another speak. If the weather's nice and you have an appropriate location, those teams who wish can move outside for the role-playing portion of the exercise.

Materials
- Flip chart paper and markers
- Completed Prospect Form (page 109)
- Sample gifts charts (pages 90-91) or a gift chart you've prepared specifically for your fundraising campaign
- Handout: Face to Face Fundraising: Structuring the Meeting (pages 140-141)

FACILITATING THE EXERCISE

1. In advance of the session, prepare two flip chart pages. On one page write:

    Structure of the Donor Meeting
      A. Briefly build rapport
      B. State your goals for the meeting

C. Uncover the prospect's interests
D. Make a brief presentation
E. Ask for the gift
F. Uncover any objections
G. Close the meeting
H. Report to the office

On the second page, draw a triangle and then at the corner of each triangle write the words *Asker, Prospect,* and *Observer.* Below the triangle, write the following:

1-2 minutes	Set up the roles
5-6 minutes	Role play
4-5 minutes	Debrief in your small group

2. Make sure your participants have already completed the ABCs of Identifying Prospects exercise on pages 106 and filled out the prospect form on page 109.

3. As you begin the exercise, ask your trainees to form groups of three. If both board and staff are participating, it's helpful to have a mix of board and staff in each triad.

4. Explain the roles to be played:

    The asker. A board member, volunteer, or staff member who helps with fundraising.
    The prospect. A current or prospective donor who is known to the Asker—in other words, he or she has a direct personal relationship.
    The observer. The team member who gets to watch and comment after the role play is complete.

    By the end of the exercise, everyone will have the opportunity to play all three roles.

    Note: If you form triads and one or two people still remain, this exercise works with groups of four—you'll have an extra observer in each group, and therefore the exercise will take a little longer.

5. Explain the specifics of each role by reading aloud the descriptions below.

    Asker – your goal is to:
    A. Introduce the work of your organization.

B. Find out, through asking questions, what the prospect cares about and how your work might address his or her interests.

C. Encourage the prospect to agree to a next step:
- Make a gift or a pledge *(this is the primary purpose of the meeting, so start here)*
- Schedule a follow-up meeting with the prospect's partner or spouse
- Suggest other prospects
- Volunteer to help with program or fundraising needs

Prospect – your goal is to:
A. Learn more about this group without spending a lot of time.

B. If you can, identify one aspect of the group, the project, or the presentation that catches your attention.

C. Provide two or three objections or obstacles for the solicitor to address.

D. Based on the conversation, decide if you will:
- Contribute or pledge today
- Delay your decision ("I'd like to think about it")
- Decline to donate
- Become involved in some other way

Observer – your goal is to watch, listen, take notes, and be prepared to comment on what you see and hear during the debriefing period.

6. With the group, review the flip chart notes describing the structure of the meeting, talking your group through the specifics. You can augment this conversation by distributing the handout Face-to-Face Fundraising: Structuring the Meeting on pages 140-141.

7. To begin the role play, the trios divide up the roles for the first round. The asker reviews his or her completed prospect form (page 109) and chooses one person on the list, or simply picks someone in real life that he or she hopes to solicit. The asker then trains the prospect to "be" that person during the role play. This doesn't require a full biography or complete history with the organization—just a few pertinent notes.

For example, the asker might say to the prospect, "For the role play, I want you to be my Aunt Rita. She always asks about my work and seems interested. She came to our open house last year but has never given. When I was at the theatre I saw her listed in the program as a $500 donor, and she is also active in her church, so I know she's a 'giver.' Let me tell you a little more about her …"

8. Explain the debriefing model before beginning the role play, using the second flip chart page you prepared in advance. After each round, the trio debriefs the exercise as follows:

- The asker goes first. He or she says two things about the meeting that went well (two compliments) and one suggestion for how to improve it. For example, "I was enthusiastic and I know the organization really well, but then I asked for the money and kept talking. I need to ask and have the discipline to be quiet."
- The prospect goes next, following the same format: providing two compliments to the asker and one suggestion.
- Finally, the observer offers comments, following the same format: two compliments and one suggestion for the asker.

9. Each round of this exercise—dividing up the roles, doing the role play, and debriefing—takes about 15 minutes. Then all participants rotate to a new role. As the facilitator, keep general track of the time (you don't need to ring a bell every 15 minutes), check in with the groups occasionally, and speed them up or slow them down as needed.

10. To debrief this exercise, reconvene the full group and ask some combination of the following questions:

- What did you learn from this exercise?
- When you were the asker, what's one thing you did well?
- What do you need to improve on?
- What do you want to remember from this exercise to use the next time you ask for a gift?

TRAINING TIP Many are visual learners, grasping concepts more effectively through pictures and symbols, which is why we asked you to create the triangle with the words Asker, Prospect, and Observer. This simple graphic, paired with the number of minutes for each portion of the exercise, makes it easier to understand how the exercise is supposed to work.

Stop-Action Soliciting

There's something empowering about being able to try an idea, rewind, and try it again—or to stop, ask the assembled group what to do, and then experiment with their suggestions. Stop-action exercises are a lot of fun and remarkably instructive. This activity offers a mix of observing others and active participation. You'll need to recruit a trustee or staff member with experience asking for gifts and who is willing to conduct a mock solicitation in front of (and with the collective advice of) members of the group.

Why Do This Exercise?
Your trainees can observe effective solicitor behavior (or not) while having the opportunity to intervene and improve that behavior

Use This Exercise When
Your solicitors have completed a few donor visits and are ready to work through any challenges or opportunities that emerged during those conversations

Time Required
45-60 minutes, depending on the number of donor meetings

Audience
Anyone involved with your fundraising campaign who will participate in donor visits: some combination of board, staff, and volunteers

Setting
A room large enough to place chairs in a semicircle with two chairs in the front facing one another

Materials
A Donor Profile Form (see page 154) for each round of the exercise.

FACILITATING THE EXERCISE

1. In advance, select up to three donors who have different personal characteristics and relationships with your organization. For example, one donor might be a retired woman who has volunteered with your organization and has given multiple small gifts over many years. For each person, fill out the Donor Profile Form on page 154. To preserve confidentiality, we suggest you change the names and any unique characteristics that might identify these people. Make copies to share with your participants.

2. Recruit two volunteers beforehand: one to play the donor and the other the solicitor. It might be helpful to meet in advance to review the profile and talk through the exercise. You can use the same volunteers for more

than one role play, or recruit new volunteers for subsequent rounds. In either case, the solicitor should have some fundraising experience and know the basics of asking for a gift.

3. Ask the two volunteers to sit at the front of the room. Distribute the first donor profile to all participants and review it together, encouraging questions about the donor. The person playing the donor should feel free to improvise, adding details to the role as he or she sees fit.

4. Tell the group that they're about to watch a donor being solicited. Two or three times during the process, either the asker or the facilitator will stop the action and seek advice from the group. For example, if the asker isn't sure how to respond to something the donor has said, he or she can stop, poll the group, and then the solicitation resumes. Or the facilitator might stop the action and say to the participants, "How would you handle this situation?" In some cases, the solicitor might return to an earlier point in the conversation and redirect it based on advice from the group.

5. We recommend no more than three stops per meeting. At the conclusion of each role play, ask the participants what worked well and specifically what techniques or approaches they might use when meeting with donors. The group can call for a rewind to try a different approach.

6. If you're doing more than one round of mock donor meetings, recruit volunteers for subsequent rounds. If there are no willing recruits, stay with the same volunteers.

7. To debrief this exercise, ask some combination of the following questions:

   - What challenges are you most likely to face in your own donor meetings? What solutions did you learn today that you can apply?
   - If we needed a stop-action "do-over" during an actual donor meeting, how might we ask for it?

TRAINING TIP As a facilitator, your job is to create the opportunity for participants to raise difficult questions and address challenging moments. If no one steps up, you may need to raise these questions yourself. What if the donor says something offensive—how would you respond? Or if she keeps changing the subject? Or if the prospect drops a hint the solicitor misses? Remember, the point of this exercise is to solve problems by deconstructing donor meetings—so make sure that a few challenges and/ or opportunities are built into each scenario.

Donor Profile Form

Name of donor or prospect:

Approximate age:

Family:

Biographical information:

Businesses and business relationships:

Special interests:

Other identifying characteristics:

Giving history:
- Your organization:

- Other organizations:

Goal of donor meeting:

PART 7

AFTER THE ASK

Whew! You asked Joan for a gift and she said yes. Congratulations! Job well done. You may be thinking, okay, now it's time to talk to Joe.

Slow down. Your relationship with Joan is just getting interesting.

It's natural to view asking as an end point. When it's done, there's a tendency to check off that person and move to the next prospect. But fundraising isn't about money, it's about relationships—and in some ways, the relationship begins with the gift. Asking for money can feel daunting, but thanking people for their generosity and learning more about their interests and passions is perhaps the most inspiring, essential, and rewarding aspect of fundraising.

In this chapter, we focus on the importance of seeing the gift as a beginning rather than the end.

If your board members didn't participate in soliciting donors—don't feel bad, this is a challenge for many, many boards—use these exercises to encourage them to jump in *now*, thanking and engaging donors more fully. With a little effort, you can move beyond the "Dear Mrs. Smith" thank you letter to a deeper model of donor appreciation and involvement.

The Gift Is Just the Beginning

 00:20

Engaging donors after they give allows you to tap into their skills and relationships and increases their commitment to your organization. By developing an "involvement menu," you can provide more opportunities for board members and other volunteers—especially those who don't want to ask for money—to participate in fundraising.

This activity builds on the Cycle of Fundraising exercise on page 41.

Why Do This Exercise? If you don't effectively engage your donors after they give, they won't give again	**Audience** Anyone involved with your fundraising campaign: some combination of board, staff, and volunteers
Use This Exercise When You want to focus attention on the best ways to thank and recognize donors	**Setting** A space large enough to accommodate several small groups of three to five each
Time Required About 20 minutes	**Materials** Flip chart paper and markers

FACILITATING THE EXERCISE

1. Ask the participants to form small groups of three to five. Their task is to brainstorm ways to involve donors once they've made a gift. Give each group about five minutes to complete this work. To provide a sense of the possibilities, here are a few examples:

    * Invite supporters to educational events
    * Ask for advice
    * Encourage them to host a house party
    * Ask for referrals and introductions
    * Ask donors to join a committee

2. Once participants have completed this task, ask them to review their lists and select their three favorites. Give them two minutes for this task.

3. Reconvene everyone and have each small group report their three best ideas, writing their answers on a sheet of flip chart paper. If participants have other favorites that didn't make the top-three list, ask for those as well.

4. Debrief the exercise using some combination of the following questions:

   - Name a few organizations that do a good job engaging their donors after they give. What can we learn from them?
   - As a donor, which of these strategies would be most appealing to you? Why?
   - How can we take this list and personalize it for each of our most generous supporters? What are our next steps? (One idea: organize a round of phone calls or visit with donors to share the list and ask if and how they would like to be more involved.)

TRAINING TIP Here's a famous fundraising mantra: "If you want advice, ask for money. If you want money, ask for advice." If you would like to expand this exercise, brainstorm a list of questions you could ask donors to elicit their feedback on your programs, long-range plan, and fundraising opportunities.

Your Favorite Thanks

 `00:30`

Fundraising is about gratitude and appreciation. When we demonstrate genuine, personal appreciation, donors respond —and they keep giving. By developing a "thank you menu," you can provide more opportunities for board members and other volunteers (especially those who don't want to ask for money) to participate in fundraising in a way that's significant to both the donor and your organization.

Why Do This Exercise?
To develop a culture of gratitude within your organization

Use This Exercise When
You're preparing for face-to-face asks—because you need to have a donor-recognition plan in place *before* you solicit a single gift

Time Required
About 30 minutes

Audience
Anyone involved with your donor campaign: some combination of board, staff, and volunteers

Setting
A space large enough to accommodate several small groups of three to five each

Materials
Flip chart paper and markers

FACILITATING THE EXERCISE

1. Ask your colleagues to form small groups of three to five to discuss and answer the following question: "Have you ever been thanked in a meaningful way? This could include thanks for a charitable donation, but don't limit yourself. What were your most meaningful thank you experiences?"

2. After five to ten minutes, reconvene the large group and on flip chart paper list their responses: personal thanks, handwritten notes, public recognition, flowers, and so forth.

3. Using this list, initiate a conversation about the ways your organization might create a plan for thanking donors. Begin by asking participants' opinions about how many times a donor should be thanked after making a gift. (Note: the industry standard is seven thanks, using a variety of ways, for each gift.) The point of this question isn't to argue about the correct number but to talk about why sending the traditional, formal thank you letter—and then forgetting about the donor—is bad policy.

4. Briefly describe one of your major donors, writing his or her name at the top of a flip chart page. Ask the group to help you develop a "thank you plan" for that donor, brainstorming a series of steps you could take to show appreciation. For example, "Simon has given $2,500 each year for several years. He's sort of introverted but seems to light up when you ask him questions. His wife, Carmen, is the opposite—very outgoing, loves parties, gets a little uncomfortable if you ask her too much about herself. What thank you plan would work best for them?"

5. Next, describe a mid-level donor and put his or her name on another page. Ask the group to develop a "thank you plan" for this contributor.

6. If you wish, you can do the same with a low-level donor. By developing plans for thanking donors who give at different levels, the group will begin to think strategically about where to invest time and attention.

7. Debrief the exercise using some combination of the following questions:

    *   What do the most meaningful thanks have in common?
    *   In what ways is this exercise an antidote to "donor fatigue?"
    *   If thanking is easier than asking, why do so many nonprofits do an inadequate job of it?

TRAINING TIP As you're setting up this exercise, begin with a personal story of how you (or a family member, or a friend) have been thanked in a meaningful way. Andy often tells a story about his father talking to a group of schoolchildren about his experiences in World War II and then receiving a folder of hand-written thank you notes from the kids. To emphasize that this brainstorm isn't just about charitable gifts, tell a story of gratitude that has nothing to do with giving money to a nonprofit organization.

Thanking Donors from A to Z

Researchers like Penelope Burk of Cygnus Applied Research have demonstrated that donors don't respond very well to the typical thank you: the impersonal, predictable form letter, filled with stock phrases, that's automatically generated from a database. These letters are perhaps a necessary step—they provide a receipt for those who itemize their tax deductions—but they don't convey gratitude in a personal way.

With this exercise, you can have fun brainstorming creative ways to thank people. By thinking more broadly, you're likely to inspire a more personal touch of gratitude.

Why Do This Exercise?
The more options for thanking a donor, the better

Use This Exercise When
Your organization is stuck in a "thank you" rut

Time Required
About 20 minutes

Audience
Anyone involved with your fundraising campaign: some combination of board, staff, and volunteers

Setting
A space large enough to accommodate several small groups of three to five each

Materials
- Flip chart paper and markers (optional)
- Paper and pens
- Optional: a prize for a member of the winning team

FACILITATING THE EXERCISE

1. Ask your colleagues to form small groups of three to five. Their job is to develop a list of twenty-six ways to thank a donor, each one representing a different letter of the alphabet. Provide a few examples. One group we worked with came up with:

   J for homemade *jam*
   S for writing a *song* about the donor
   Z for a trip to the *zoo*

2. After five to ten minutes, reconvene the large group and go through the alphabet letter by letter, hearing each idea. If you wish, you can write the list on the flip chart.

3. Ask the group to suggest a handful of ideas from the exercise that might be appropriate for your organization. Recruit a team of volunteers to work with you—at a later date—on developing a plan to implement these ideas with your donors.

4. Debrief the exercise using some combination of the following questions.

   - Which suggestion is your favorite? Why?
   - If we haven't been this creative with our thank yous in the past, why not? How do we change our culture to be more creative?
   - If you can, name one donor and match the donor with one of these ideas. Why did you make that match?

TRAINING TIP By turning a small-group exercise into a friendly competition, you can increase the energy in the room. In this case, you can offer a prize to the group that completes the alphabet first. Everyone in the winning group gets a slip of paper on which to write their name. Pick a winner. Provide an appropriate prize: a meal at your favorite restaurant, a book (a fundraising book?), a favorite local food, perhaps a T-shirt or coffee mug from your organization.

After the Yes: Questions You Can Ask Donors

If you and your colleagues are new to face-to-face fundraising, you're probably focusing on "the ask" and how to frame your request in the most compelling, inspiring way. Without a doubt, a strong pitch is one of the keys to successful fundraising—but then what? When you hear the words "Yes, I'd like to help," how do you respond? This exercise will help you develop a set of follow-up questions to better serve your donors and strengthen these relationships.

In the accompanying handouts, we've included several sample questions with the caution that not every question applies to every donor or every visit. This is a conversation or perhaps a negotiation—not an interrogation. Choose the questions that seem most relevant and adapt them to your needs and circumstances.

Why Do This Exercise?
To emphasize fundraising is about serving the donor—and if you don't know what the donor wants, you can't provide good service

Use This Exercise When
You and your team are comfortable with "the ask" and you're ready to focus on the next steps you can take with your donors

Time Required
About 20 minutes

Audience
Anyone involved with your fundraising campaign: some combination of board, staff, and volunteers

Setting
A space large enough to accommodate several small groups of three to five each

Materials
- After the Yes: Sample Questions (pages 164-165)
- After the Yes: Donor Tracking Form (pages 166-167)

FACILITATING THE EXERCISE

1. In advance, make photocopies of the handouts listed above.

2. Ask your colleagues to form small groups of three to five per group to discuss and answer the following question: "When you meet with a donor and he or she makes a verbal commitment—'Yes, I'd like to give'—what

follow-up questions should you ask after thanking the donor for his or her gift?" As an example, you might offer the following question: "May we include your name in our published list of donors, or would you prefer to be anonymous?"

3. After five to ten minutes, distribute the handout "After the Yes: Sample Questions" on pages 164-165. Instruct the groups to compare their questions with the ones included in the handout. Which ones are similar? Did they come up with any questions not included in the handout?

4. After a minute, distribute the handout "After the Yes: Donor Tracking Form" on pages 166-167. Give everyone a minute or two to look it over, explaining that the work from this exercise can be captured in a tracking form to use when talking with donors. Take questions as needed.

5. Debrief the exercise using some combination of the following questions:

   • From your perspective, which of these questions are most important? Why?
   • How would you present these questions without making the donor feel like it's an interrogation?
   • As a donor yourself, what is the most meaningful thing an organization can do after you give?

This exercise is adapted from an article that first appeared in the Grassroots Fundraising Journal, www.grassrootsfundraising.org. Many thanks to our colleague and article co-author Harvey McKinnon.

TRAINING TIP One way to stimulate discussion is to reverse roles and say to your colleagues, "Imagine that you're the donor. You've just been solicited for a significant donation and agreed to give. What questions would you like to be asked in that moment?"

After the Yes

SAMPLE QUESTIONS

Here are several "after questions" we like, with follow-up language included. Choose the ones that are most relevant to the donor and the situation.

Note: When a donor says yes, offer a warm thank you and talk a little about how the gift will be meaningful to meeting the organization's mission before continuing with the questions below.

- "How would you like to pay? Do you want to write a check now? Would you like us to send you a pledge statement in the mail? If you're interested in our sustainer program, you can fulfill your pledge in automatic monthly installments."

- "How do you want us to use this gift?" Check your notes from this meeting and all previous conversations with the donor. If you sense any indications that he or she wants to restrict his or her gift to a specific program or campaign, this is the time to clarify and honor that intent.

- "How would you like to be recognized? We publish donor names in our newsletter, our annual report, and on our website. We'd love to include your name so we can publicly express our thanks … and your commitment will inspire other people to give. May we list your name, or would you prefer to be anonymous?" Check the spelling with the donor.

- "Do you want your gift to honor someone you care about? We can list their name, your name, or both."

- "Tell me a little more about why you support our work. We're always interested in what motivates our donors to give; this helps us reach out to other potential donors. You just made a very generous decision—I'd really appreciate knowing why."

- "Would you be willing to give a testimonial we can use in our newsletter and other promotional materials? May we include your photo? Our most generous supporters —people like you—are our most credible advocates. May we have a sentence or two to inspire others?"

- "Would you be willing to join us at a board meeting and talk about why you support our work? It's really helpful for the board to hear directly from donors—it reminds them why we do the work we do and why it's important to ask people to contribute. It will inspire them to work harder in support of our mission. Would you share your experience with the board?"

- "How would you like to be kept informed about our work—and how often? Do you want a printed newsletter or do you prefer brief emails? Shall I phone you from time to time? Do you use social media like Facebook? Would you prefer to receive updates in person and, if so, how many times per year?"

- "When I come back to give you a progress report, would you be willing to include family members so they can learn about what your support makes possible?" If you're cultivating donors for future gifts, especially planned gifts, this is an essential step.

- "Can you recommend other people we can talk to about a gift? Do you have friends or colleagues who might want to join you in supporting our work? Would you be willing to make an introduction—by phone, by email, or in person—or join me for the initial visit?"

- "Given your strong commitment to our work, would you consider volunteering to help us raise money? For example, would you be willing to come along when I meet with prospects and talk about why you give?"

- "What's your personal giving calendar? Are you typically a once-a-year donor? Twice a year? If we have an urgent need, can we approach you again? What schedule works best for you?"

After the Yes

DONOR TRACKING FORM

Donor name(s) _____

Date of conversation _____

Terms of gift and payment schedule

Full payment now

__ Check

__ Credit card   Visa/MC/Amex #_____ Expiration ___/___

__ Securities or other

Notes:

Pledge

Payments will be made

____ Once per year on _____ (date)

____ Twice per year on _____ and _____ (dates)

____ Four times per year on _____, _____, _____, and _____ (dates)

____ Monthly

Notes:

Use of gift

__ Unrestricted

__ Restricted to _____

Notes:

1. **Recognition**

    __ Would like to be recognized in our publications *(confirm correct spelling of name)*

    __ Would prefer to remain anonymous

    Notes:

2. **Honor or remember**

    __ Gift in honor of _____

    __ Gift in memory of _____

    Notes:

3. **Why does the donor support our work?**

4. **Willing to give written testimonial?**
   __ Yes   __ No
   Notes:

5. **Willing to talk with board about why he/she supports our work?**
   __ Yes   __ No
   Notes:

6. **Communication preferences – note top three in order of preference**
   __ Personal meeting   How often? _____
   __ Phone call   How often? _____
   __ Email   How often? _____
   __ Social media   How often? _____
   __ Newsletter   How often? _____
   __ Personal note/letter   How often? _____
   __ Website   How often? _____
   __ Other (describe)   How often? _____

7. **Willing to involve family members in future conversations?**
   __ Yes   __ No
   Notes:

8. **Prospect leads**
   Name _____   Contact info _____
   Name _____   Contact info _____
   Name _____   Contact info _____

9. **Potential fundraising volunteer?**
   __ Yes   __ No
   Notes:

10. **Personal giving calendar**
    __ Annual
    __ Multi-year commitment; number of years _____
    __ As needed; OK to ask more than once per year

PART 8

ASKING IN OTHER WAYS

Throughout this book, we've focused on face-to-face fundraising because:

- It's the most effective way to ask for a gift. Compared to other fundraising strategies, it generates the most money for the time, effort, and money you invest.
- It's also the scariest way to ask for a gift, which is why training, practice, and role plays are so essential.

But we're also realists. Despite the best training in the world, not every board member will embrace face-to-face fundraising, but they can and should participate in other ways.

In Part 4, we included two exercises—Creating a Board Fundraising Menu and Building a Board Fundraising Ladder—to help you identify a variety of options for engaging your trustees. This section features several additional strategies you can use with your board and other volunteers.

Planning a Fundraising House Party

At some point in our lives, most of us have organized a party. This strategy takes something we already know how to do and adds a fundraising component. House parties are fun, relatively easy to organize, and a good way to recruit board members and other volunteers to help with fundraising. As with anything else, good planning saves time and aggravation, increasing your odds of success.

The exercise works well with the companion exercise, Fundraising House Parties: Engaging Your Board, on page 173.

Why Do This Exercise?
Because parties are fun and, when well-organized, can be lucrative

Use This Exercise When
You're looking for a more intimate (and less exhausting) alternative to the giant gala fundraising event

Time Required
90 minutes

Audience
The leadership team for your fundraising campaign: some combination of board, staff, and volunteers. This exercise is best done with a group of four to eight people.

Setting
A space large enough to accommodate several pairs or teams of three working together

Materials
- Flip chart paper and markers
- Handout: House Party Overview (page 172)

FACILITATING THE EXERCISE

1. In advance, photocopy the House Party Overview handout. Share the handout and discuss it with the group to ensure everyone understands the basics of a house party:

   - It's an intimate gathering, rather than a large public event.
   - These parties work best in a private home.
   - There are several models for raising money (or not) using house parties. As you plan your party, you'll need to choose the model that works best for you.

2. Ask your colleagues to gather in pairs or groups of three. Instruct them to review the fundraising options for a house party and create a list of pros and cons for each option, with one person in each group taking notes:

- Collect a fixed price in advance
- Ask at the event
- Treat the party as a free friend-raiser or cultivation event—with the option of following up individually with those who attend

3. After five minutes, reconvene the full group to review the list and decide which approach will work best for your party. (Note: The ask-at-the-event model is a little more challenging to organize but tends to raise the most money.) Your job is to facilitate the conversation and seek a consensus. If people have strong disagreements, suggest the following: "Let's organize more than one party using different fundraising models and then compare the results to see what worked best."

4. Talk with the group about the concept of "party hooks." The most basic hook is the chance to support a friend (the host) and learn more about an interesting cause, but there may be others. Will it be the food? The location? A chance to discuss a timely issue? A chance to meet a celebrity? The chance to make new friends?

   For example, when Andy worked at Native Seeds/SEARCH, a regional seed conservation organization in Arizona, their fundraising house parties featured gourmet menus based on traditional native foods: a unique, tasty hook. These menus were included in all event invitations.

5. Ask the small groups to gather again and brainstorm possible hooks for your house party. After about three minutes, reconvene the full group to discuss the options and decide on a hook.

6. On one sheet of flip chart paper, write the words:
       6 weeks out
       5 weeks out
       4 weeks out

   Write them with enough space between each week to fill in the details. Prepare a second sheet as follows:
       3 weeks out
       2 weeks out
       1 week out

And a third:
> Day of event
>
> After the event

Use the same spacing as the first sheet, leaving room to add details.

7. The full group brainstorms a list of tasks needed to organize a party—identify a host or host committee, prepare invitations, arrange for food, and the like—while the facilitator writes these tasks on the flip chart under the relevant week. Most of these tasks are self-evident, because house party planning builds on common wisdom. Anyone who's ever organized a baby shower, anniversary event, or birthday party will have a good sense of the work to be done.

   When the flip chart pages are filled in, your calendar is complete. You can use this calendar to create a spreadsheet to guide the work of the party planning team. You can also keep the large calendar handy to post at planning committee meetings to stay on task.

8. To debrief this exercise, use some combination of the following questions:

- What's one thing you've learned from past experience that we need to remember as we're planning this party?
- What are our next steps?
- Who will do what? By when?

An excellent resource is The Fundraising Houseparty by Morrie Warshawski, www.warshawski.com.

> **TRAINING TIP** The success of this exercise depends completely on who participates, so make sure your planning team includes a few people who love everything about parties: planning them, attending them, talking about them, analyzing what makes them work. Their enthusiasm will be infectious.

House Party Overview

Defined

- Intimate; 15 to 50 people
- In a private home
- Brief; 2 hours maximum. Includes a 10-15 minute presentation and (perhaps) an ask; see below
- Quick to organize; 4-6 weeks to plan and do
- Volunteer-driven

Decision points

1. Host or host committee
2. Venue (whose home?)
3. Fundraising goal; typically $2,500 - $10,000
4. "Hook"—What will attract the participants? A celebrity? Menu? Venue? A request from a friend?
5. Invitation list
   - 25-40 percent of invitees will attend *if you phone them* after sending the invitation
   - 50/50 model: Half the list from host, half from the organization
6. How to ask for the gift
   - Fixed price in advance
   - Ask at the event (most efficient for time spent)
   - Treat it as a "friend-raiser" and follow up individually with those who attend
7. Who asks?
   - The host
   - Someone introduced by the host

Fundraising House Parties: Engaging Your Board

Good party planning involves a wide range of tasks, nearly all of which can be done by volunteers. Use this exercise to develop a party-planning menu for your board. If you like, you can structure it as a contest with prizes, which generates more excitement.

This activity nicely augments Planning a Fundraising House Party on page 169.

Why Do This Exercise?
It builds on common expertise: how to organize a party

Use This Exercise When
You're looking for new ways to involve your board, especially those who enjoy a good party

Time Required
30 minutes

Audience
The leadership team for your fundraising campaign: some combination of board, staff, and volunteers

Setting
A space large enough to accommodate several small groups of 3-5 people each with some privacy

Materials
- Stopwatch or timer
- Bell or whistle (optional)
- Flip chart paper and markers
- Handout: House Party Overview (page 172)
- Optional: a prize for a member of the winning team

FACILITATING THE EXERCISE

1. In advance, photocopy the House Party Overview handout. Share the handout and discuss it with the group to ensure everyone understands the basics of a house party:

   - It's an intimate gathering, rather than a large public event.
   - These parties work best in a private home—hence the term "house party."

- There are several models for raising money (or not) using house parties. As you plan your party, you'll need to choose the model that works best for you.

2. Sort the participants into small groups of four to eight each. Provide each group with a piece of flip chart paper and several markers and have them move to different corners of the room so they can have privacy while brainstorming.

3. Provide the following instructions: "Your job is to brainstorm all the different ways board members or other volunteers can assist with planning and delivering a fundraising house party. You can include big-picture tasks, such as creating the planning calendar, all the way down to micro-tasks, like preparing name tags. Use the markers to write your ideas on the flip chart. More than one person can write on the flip chart.

   "You'll have three minutes to complete this brainstorm. This is a contest: the group originating the most items in three minutes will be entered into a drawing to win a fabulous prize. Any questions? Okay, on your mark … get set … go!"

4. When about a minute remains, you can shout out, "One minute! One minute to go!" If you sense a lot of energy in the room—if the groups are continuing to generate new ideas—let the exercise run more than three minutes (no one else will be keeping time) but DO NOT let it drag on.

5. Ask each group to select a spokesperson who will report the items on their list.

6. Reconvene everyone into the large group to hear these reports and take notes on the flip chart. Here are some unexpected but helpful tasks you might want to add to your list.

   - Arrange transportation/designated driver
   - Arrange child care
   - Take photos for your newsletter, Facebook page, blog
   - Write a newsletter article after the event
   - Arrange for host/hostess gift
   - Clean the house both before and after the event
   - "Work the room"—make introductions
   - Park cars (this is essential in some neighborhoods)
   - Gather after the guests have gone and share anything you learned that

might be helpful

- Thank you calls to attendees
- Identify a host (or member of the host committee) for the next party

7. Identify a volunteer who will transcribe the flip chart notes (or take a photo of these notes) for later use with your party-planning team.

8. Ask each group to shout out the total number of items in their brainstorm. Everyone in the winning group receives a slip of paper on which to write their name; then pick a winner. Provide an appropriate prize: a meal at your favorite restaurant, a book (a fundraising book?), a favorite local food, perhaps a T-shirt or coffee mug from your organization.

9. To debrief this exercise, ask some combination of the following questions:

- What is one task that you would be willing to do to support a party?
- Are we ready to include house party participation in our list of board expectations? If so, how do we proceed?
- Is anyone present willing to serve on the planning team?
- Is anyone present willing to host a party?

TRAINING TIP We all land on different places along the introvert-extrovert continuum. If you have a small group filled with introverts, they'll have a harder time with this exercise because they may not like parties or even small group activities. Don't obsess over this, but to the degree you can blend a mix of introverts and extroverts in your work groups, everyone will have more fun with this exercise, and you'll get better results.

Pitching in Public

Faced with a crowd of expectant people, a few fearless souls can improvise a compelling fundraising pitch. The rest of us are likely to feel intimidated by the idea of facing a group and talking about anything ... especially money.

As we've noted in previous exercises, the most effective fundraising house parties include an ask: a direct appeal to partygoers to support the organization. This exercise will help you strengthen your pitch and increase your confidence.

Why Do This Exercise?
At most events, you have one opportunity to make a pitch—so you might as well do a good job

Use This Exercise When
You're planning a house party or other public event that includes a direct appeal for funds

Time Required
45 minutes

Audience
Anyone involved with your fundraising campaign: some combination of board, staff, and volunteers

Setting
A space large enough to accommodate several small groups of three each

Materials
Public Pitch worksheet (page 178)

FACILITATING THE EXERCISE

1. Photocopy the worksheet on page 178 in advance.

2. Hand out copies of the worksheet. Give the participants no more than ten minutes to write a sentence or two for each item on the worksheet. Reassure them this is just practice, rather than a polished presentation. If it feels helpful, talk them through each item below and give an example, modeling your own pitch.

    a) Introduce yourself: your name, organization, and your relationship to the organization
    b) Explain why the group exists or why you got involved
    c) Tell a story that gives a "face" to the problem or issue
    d) Give a statistic or fact about the problem or issue
    e) Describe what the organization is doing to address the problem
    f) Tell the audience what action you'd like them to take

Participants should imagine that they're making this pitch in front of a group of people—it could be a house party or a larger public event. The goal is to become more succinct and tell better stories, rather than just describe what the organization does.

3. Once they've finished writing, ask them to form groups of three. Let them know that each person will have two minutes to make his or her pitch. You can keep time for everyone or ask each small group to be responsible for its own time management. (If you have enough time, you can have each group do a second round of pitches, giving each person a chance to apply the lessons they learned during the first round.)

4. Speakers may use their notes, but discourage them from staring at the paper and reading what they've written. After each pitch, the speaker gets two minutes of feedback from his or her colleagues. Feedback should always include both positive comments and suggestions for improvement.

5. Reconvene the full group and ask for two or three volunteers to pitch and receive feedback from the large group. As facilitator, offer compliments and also constructive suggestions—especially if none of the participants raises a point you feel is important.

6. To debrief this exercise, ask the following questions:

    *   What did you hear that was most compelling?
    *   What are the most important components of a successful pitch?
    *   If you found this activity challenging, why? What can we do to reduce our anxiety?

We thank our colleague Stephanie Roth of Klein and Roth Consulting for sharing this exercise.

TRAINING TIP As with many role-play exercises, people like to observe someone else before doing it themselves. Prepare yourself to model an effective pitch or recruit someone in advance who will do a good job and make sure that he or she prepares in advance.

Public Pitch Worksheet

a) Introduce yourself: your name, organization, and your relationship to the organization

b) Explain why the group exists or why you got involved

c) Tell a story that gives a "face" to the problem or issue

d) Give a statistic or fact about the problem or issue

e) Describe what the organization is doing to address the problem

f) Tell the audience what action you'd like them to take

Asking For Goods and Services

 00:30

In the words of author and consultant Gayle Gifford, who shared this exercise, "Many people feel more comfortable asking for stuff than asking for money—and if it comes off a budget line, it's as good as cash." This exercise engages your fundraising team in thinking about the types of non-cash (also known as in-kind) contributions that might benefit your organization and helps motivate them to go out and solicit these items.

Why Do This Exercise?
Goods and services may be as valuable as money and may be easier to ask for and to get

Use This Exercise When
You're planning a benefit auction or raffle and need prizes, or when you need specific services and products to improve your organizational effectiveness

Time Required
30 minutes

Audience
Anyone involved with your fundraising campaign: some combination of board, staff, and volunteers

Setting
A room large enough to accommodate your trainees around a table or in a circle of chairs

Materials
Flip chart paper and markers

FACILITATING THE EXERCISE

1. Ask participants to brainstorm at least ten items your organization needs—*other than money*—that someone might give. As they're brainstorming, write their answers on the flip chart, leaving space after each item. Make sure to include services—for example, Web design, accounting assistance, staff and board training—in addition to products like food and computers.

2. Once you complete the list, ask participants to imagine requesting donations of these items. Ask the following questions:

   • Are any of these items equivalent to money? If so, how?
   • How would you feel about asking for these things, as opposed to asking for money? If it feels different, how? Why?

3. Return to the list and encourage people to suggest sources to contribute items, writing them beneath the relevant items. For example, if a bicycle is on the list, you might write down local bike shops or people you know who are avid cyclists.

4. Finally, go through the list one more time and ask for volunteers to approach specific providers and ask for specific items. Write the names of these volunteers beside the people or businesses they agree to approach.

   For help with the pitch—what to say when you're asking for donated items—take a look at several other exercises in this book, including The Case, Simplified (page 67), Your One Minute of Fame (page 70) , and Pitching in Public (page 176).

5. To debrief this exercise, use some combination of the following questions:

   • If you were approached to donate goods or services, how would you feel?
   • What can we do to recognize and publicly thank those who give?
   • How can we encourage our members to support businesses that support us?

We thank our colleague Gayle Gifford for sharing this exercise.

TRAINING TIP In many communities—particularly smaller ones—fundraising equals walking down Main Street soliciting every storefront business. Because these people are asked so often, they develop skills for saying no. So it's important to encourage your participants to brainstorm a list of prospects beyond the usual suspects—for example, a friend or colleague who lives in a different community but might support your work. It's also worth stressing the importance of treating everyone with respect, especially when they decline your request.

ABOUT THE AUTHORS

Andrea Kihlstedt has served the nonprofit sector for more than thirty years as a fundraiser, trainer, consultant, teacher, writer and speaker. She has trained nonprofit boards and staff throughout the U.S. on effective major gifts fundraising, capital campaigns and how to ask for gifts.

Kihlstedt is cofounder (with Gail Perry) of Capital Campaign Magic, providing online learning about capital campaign fundraising. For more information about Capital Campaign Magic visit: http://www.capitalcampaignmagic.com/

Kihlstedt, her husband Tyko and their two cats, Hairy Potter and Shadow, live in New York City where they enjoy going to plays and concerts, walking in Central Park, and drinking good wine.

For more information on Kihlstedt's other books and her workshops, speaking and coaching, visit: www.andreakihlstedt.com.

Andy Robinson provides training and consulting for nonprofits in fundraising, grantseeking, board development, marketing, earned income, planning, leadership development, and facilitation. Over the past eighteen years, Andy has worked with organizations in 47 U.S. states and Canada.

Andy is the author of six books. His latest include *How to Raise $500 to $5000 From Almost Anyone*, *The Board Member's Easier Than You Think Guide to Nonprofit Finances*, and *Great Boards for Small Groups*, all published by Emerson & Church.

Grassroots Grants and *Selling Social Change* are available from Jossey-Bass.

When he's not on the road, Andy lives in Plainfield, Vermont with his wife Jan, a woodlot filled with wildlife, and a garden that is completely out of control.

For more information, please visit www.andyrobinsononline.com.

ACKNOWLEDGMENTS—AND A NOTE ON AUTHORSHIP

As our colleague Kim Klein points out, there are probably no original exercises. In her words, "Every exercise is built on something someone else has done or something we've seen." One of the listening exercises in Part 6 is a good example. It was adapted from a training program for hospice volunteers.

The fundraising community produces dozens of books and countless articles and blog postings each year, yet one could argue that the basic wisdom was codified decades ago, and writers like us are mostly repackaging and recycling that information. As author Joan Flanagan once said, "All the knowledge about fundraising can be summed up a few words: Ask 'em, thank 'em, ask 'em again, thank 'em again. And give money yourself." Not surprisingly, the exercises published here are about helping people increase their comfort and skill in asking, thanking, and giving.

Throughout the book, we've done our best to credit colleagues and peers for their work. In some cases, we've been using these exercises for decades and can't remember who first shared them with us. This happens when you reach a certain age.

If you feel like you originated one of these activities (or know who did), please tell us, and we'll endeavor to give appropriate credit in future editions.

We are grateful to our wonderful nonprofit colleagues who add to the common pool of fundraising wisdom and also draw from it as needed. May we all continue to freely and generously share what we know.

Many of our peers suggested exercises, critiqued an earlier draft of this book, or both. We are indebted to:

Mike Bacon, Bacon Lee & Associates
Xan Blake, The Blake Partnership
Gary Bukowski, Barber National Institute
Tina Cincotti, Funding Change Consulting
Tomijean Fernandez, American Civil Liberties Union
Gayle Gifford, Cause and Effect
Christine Graham, CPG Enterprises
Keiren Havens, Health Care for the Homeless

Susan Howlett
Priscilla Hung, Community Partners
Paul Jolly, Jump Start Growth, Inc.
Simone Joyaux, Joyaux Associates
Kim Klein, Klein and Roth Consulting
Anne Loehr, Anne Loehr & Associates
Harvey McKinnon, Harvey McKinnon Associates
Michael Miller
Gail Perry, Fired Up Fundraising
Paula Peter, The Solstice Group
Beth Raps, Raising Clarity
Mike Roque, Adobe Consulting
Stephanie Roth, Klein and Roth Consulting
Tim Seiler, The Fundraising School, Center on Philanthropy at Indiana University
Ma'ayan Simon, Converge Strategy Consulting
Betsy Steward, Westchester Children's Association
Charlie Trautman, Sciencenter
Morrie Warshawski

We would also like to acknowledge the following organizations that allowed us to share their sample materials:
Five Valleys Land Trust, Missoula, MT
Funding Change Consulting, Boston, MA
Ohio Environmental Council, Columbus, OH
North Lakeland Discovery Center, Manitowish Waters, WI
The Fundraising School, Center on Philanthropy, Indiana University, Indianapolis, IN
Toxic Action Center, Boston, MA

Copies of this and other books from the publisher are available
at discount when purchased in quantity for boards of directors
or staff.

Emerson
& Church
PUBLISHERS

15 Brook Street • Medfield, MA 02052
Tel. 508-359-0019 • Fax 508-359-2703
www.emersonandchurch.com